THE BOOK OF
Tarot

THE BOOK OF
Tarot

A spiritual key to understanding the cards

Sahar Huneidi-Palmer

SIRIUS

All images courtesy of Shutterstock

SIRIUS

This edition published in 2023 by Sirius Publishing, a division of
Arcturus Publishing Limited,
26/27 Bickels Yard, 151–153 Bermondsey Street,
London SE1 3HA

ISBN: 978-1-3988-2758-5
AD011031UK

Printed in China

Contents

CHAPTER ONE

TAROT OVERVIEW

The Book of Tarot will teach you everything you need to know to begin using the Tarot as a tool for self-development guidance and inspiration, providing definitions, methodology, and interpretations for each card, based on The Rider-Waite-Smith deck. Published in 1909, it was the first deck in English by Arthur Edward Waite, an American-born British poet, intellectual, and mystic. Pamela Colman Smith illustrated the cards, including the "pip," or Minor Arcana ones. Originally known as The Rider-Waite Tarot, it was later renamed The Rider-Waite-Smith Deck to honor her work.

The Rider-Waite-Smith marked a significant departure from preceding Tarot cards, which were mostly based on the 16th-century *Tarot of Marseilles* (the latter was used to play card games), which was the standard Tarot deck at the time. The *Marseilles* was based on Italian card decks developed in the 15th century. In this book, however, the Major Arcana sequence follows the *Tarot of Marseilles*'s order.

The Book of Tarot aims to demonstrate how the Tarot can assist your development and transform your experiences into wisdom. The process is depicted by the journey of The Fool, the first card of the Tarot, who undergoes a transformative journey to awaken his consciousness. Viewing the Tarot as a journey helps you remember the cards' sequence and the significance of their numbers, meanings and interpretations.

What is the Tarot?

Today's Tarot is one of the most popular and sophisticated divination systems.

Divination is defined by *Encyclopedia Britannica* as "the process of finding the hidden meaning or origin of events and occasionally foretelling the future." In ancient Rome, however, divination was about discovering the "will of the gods." Even though scholars now do not confine the word to its original meaning, it conveys seeking guidance from higher realms.

The Tarot is a comprehensive guidance system because of the deck's evolution. It evokes interpretations on several levels, from the mundane to the spiritual. Consulting the Tarot offers perspective, guidance, and a context for insights into real-life situations. Using the Tarot in this way assists your decision-making. Moreover, context for guidance is determined by the way the cards are laid. There are numerous ways to lay out the cards,

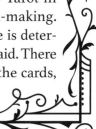

known as a "spread," in which the placement of any card has a meaning.

Each spread weaves the tapestry of your life. It can also reflect issues you need to work on, as well as what's in your subconscious. You are encouraged to create your own spreads. With practice, you will get to know the cards well, and your deck will become like a trusted friend.

The Tarot

MAJOR ARCANA

Generally, the 22 Major cards reflect the human psyche as well as the stages of a person's development. They represent major changes and turning points, while the Minor cards depict daily activities and situations. Major cards are titled as well as numbered; the title is a description of the figure on the card, such as The Magician, The Hanged Man or Strength. The Major cards serve as the foundation for interpreting the Tarot cards, symbolizing the path of personal development, enlightenment, and self-awakening. Major cards also represent an important person to the reader or the querent (the person asking for the reading) at the time of the reading and indicate the beginning of new cycles and significant transitions in the person's life, as follows:

The Fool (0), The Magician (1), The High Priestess (2), The Empress (3), The Emperor (4), The Hierophant (5), The Lovers (6), The Chariot (7), Justice (8), The Hermit (9), Wheel of Fortune (10), Strength (11), The Hanged Man (12), Death (13), Temperance (14), The Devil (15), The Tower (16), The Star (17), The Moon (18), The Sun (19), Judgment (20) and The World (21).

If you're new to the Tarot, it's a good idea to get to know the Major cards first, before you start adding the Minor cards in Tarot spreads. This method will provide a structure to your readings by presenting the general picture first, followed by details or solutions. If, for example, The Tower card comes up in a spread, it will indicate sudden upheaval. You will know that a cycle of stability might suddenly change. When following it with the Minor cards, the Five of Cups, for example, might be associated with The Tower. You might discover that the reason for (and solution to) this upheaval is your emotional attitude. The Five of Cups indicates that it is time to stop "crying over spilled milk" and move forward, toward better opportunities of which you are not even aware (see the sections Tarot Spreads and Sample Readings for more details).

CARD	NUMBER	INTERPRETATION	REVERSED MEANING
THE FOOL	0	Taking a risk, start of a new endeavor, new cycle	Foolishness, bad risk
THE MAGICIAN	1	The initiator, creative and logical	Confusion, disorganized mind
THE HIGH PRIESTESS	2	Intuition, the unknown	Self-delusion
THE EMPRESS	3	Abundance, potential fulfilled	Limited abundance
THE EMPEROR	4	Structure and authority	Disorganized, stern, inflexible
THE HIEROPHANT	5	Higher mind, innate spiritual understanding	Materialistic
THE LOVERS	6	Partnerships (romantic or business), decision	Dysfunctional partnership, indecisiveness
THE CHARIOT	7	Efforts rewarded, victory	Lack of control
JUSTICE	8	Prudence, legal matters	Dissolution of agreements
THE HERMIT	9	Inner wisdom, the teacher	Introversion
WHEEL OF FORTUNE	10	Unexpected change	Negative cycle
STRENGTH	11	Mastering spirit-matter, self-healer	Inability to control passion
THE HANGED MAN	12	Surrender, sacrifice the "old"	Useless sacrifice, waiting over
DEATH	13	Death of the old, birth of the new, end/loss	Fear of change
TEMPERANCE	14	Harmony, resolution of conflict	Imbalance
THE DEVIL	15	Enslaved to obsession, lust, restrictions	End of restraints, beginning of flow
THE TOWER	16	Sudden upheaval, destruction of the old	Disruptive behavior
THE STAR	17	Hope, bliss, optimism	Let go of doubt
THE MOON	18	Illusion, the unconscious, the unknown	Self-deception
THE SUN	19	Joy, success	Success awaits
JUDGMENT	20	Total transformation	Forced changes
THE WORLD	21	Fulfillment	Recognition awaits

Figure 1 Major Arcana key interpretations and numerology

The Drama of the Tarot

When you lay out the cards in a spread, the Major cards have a way of drawing your attention to what you need to give importance to. A card or two will always pop out at you to communicate a message. The most feared cards are possibly The Devil, Death, and Judgment. However, their images are dramatic to convey a crucial transformative message: "You are stuck in a situation that you have outgrown; your emotions are getting the worst of you."

Foretold events or cycle outcomes are not always as dramatic as they may seem. You must, however, pay attention to such cards, because they signify a turning point. When shuffling at the start of a reading, one technique to highlight those turning points is to reverse two Major and five Minor cards before you lay out the cards. If they show up in a reading, pay attention to them.

Reversed Meanings

When ominous cards appear reversed (upside down) in a reading, they have a more positive meaning—for instance, The Hanged Man and The Devil. The first reversed denotes the end of a waiting period. The Devil reversed signifies that you are about to be released from "bondage;" Death reversed suggests your unwillingness to embrace changes; and Judgment reversed denotes that you are undergoing a metamorphosis and there's nothing you can do about it!

By the time you've learned the meaning of each Tarot card in Chapter Two, you will be prepared to start reading them as you learn about spreads in Chapter Four. To arrive at the meaning of any reversed card, consider its upright qualities and attributes, and what happens to them when the card is turned upside down. Which objects would fall off? This might help trigger your own interpretations of the card in a spread. Below is a quick key interpretation of each card in upright and reversed position:

THE MINOR ARCANA SUITS

The Minor Arcana are 56 cards that are divided into four suits (Wands, Cups, Swords, and Pentacles) and show people in everyday situations. The person in the image is usually holding a tool, such as a Pentacle (money), Wand (drive), Cup

SUIT	ELEMENT	SEASON/ TIMING	KEYWORD	INTERPRETATION/ QUALITIES	CORRESPONDING PLAYING-CARD SUIT	RIDER-WAITE-SMITH SUITS
Wands	Fire	Spring	Ideas	Male aspect, inspiration, initiation, renewal, manifestation of ideas, growth. Communication and self-expression.	♣	 ACE OF WANDS
Cups	Water	Summer	Emotions	Female aspect. Emotions, creativity, happiness, love, intuition, acceptance, flow, the need for emotional support.	♥	 ACE OF CUPS
Swords	Air	Autumn	Thoughts	Sharp mind, mental activity, intellect, logical thinking, decisions that shape ideas.	♠	 ACE OF SWORDS
Pentacles	Earth	Winter	Finance	Material manifestation of creation. Money, material wealth, success, business, physical body, foundation, property.	♦	 ACE OF PENTACLES

Figure 2 The four suits and corresponding elements

(emotions) or Sword (swift, decisive action). The tool represents one of the elements of nature and denotes the suit to which the card belongs. Each suit has ten numbered "pips" cards, the first of which is known as the Ace; the remainder are numbered from 2 to 10. The Page (or Princess), Knight (or Prince), Queen, and King are the next four Royal Court Cards in each suit. Each suit has a ruling element that corresponds to the four elements of nature and carries specific attributes:

Wands symbolize the element of fire and represent drive (self-motivation). They relate to initiative and growth energy. They signify innovative thinking, innate creativity, and the ability to start new undertakings. They represent the yang aspect, or the masculine aspect of energy. They are associated with springtime because they symbolize growth. In a modern playing-card deck, the suit of clubs is their counterpart.

Cups symbolize the element of water and represent emotions. Cups represent love, happiness, and feelings. They are associated with fertility, children, beauty, relationships, and emotions toward, or inflected by, other people. The subconscious and intuition are also represented by cups since they reflect fluctuating emotions and innate senses rather than intellect or reason. As such, they represent the yin aspect, or the feminine. Cups represent summer. The suit of hearts is the modern-day equivalent.

Swords symbolize the element of air and depict intellect, mental state, and decisions. Conflict, aggression, force, ambition, strife, deception, treachery, and hatred are all represented by swords. They show "quick" actions as well as thoughts (which led to the actions) that can be positive or bad, deliberate or rash. Both sides are portrayed in the cards of this Minor Arcana suit. Swords represent autumn. Spades is their equivalent in playing cards.

Pentacles symbolize the earth element and represent money, financial matters, and material gain. The first symbol featured in the Tarot is coins, which are represented by pentacles. They are linked to financial and property interests. They were previously represented as discs or coins in Tarot decks. In everyday life, the coins signify the "fruits of labor," that is, every activity has a return or result. Pentacles are related to physical health (without which you cannot earn money). In a modern playing-card deck, the suit of pentacles corresponds to diamonds. Pentacles represent winter.

THE FOUR ELEMENTS

The Tarot and conventional playing cards have similarities that come from their shared roots. One of these is the deck's division into four suits. While the names of Tarot suits vary from deck to deck, the most common names for them are Swords (Blades, sometimes Crystals), Wands (Staves, Rods), Cups and Pentacles (Coins or Disks). These suits are essentially like standard decks of playing cards. Enigmatically, however, the order of the cards, as well as the four suits they consisted of, have remained unchanged since about the 14th century.

Wands represent Fire: The masculine principle of "taking initiative" or drive. Wands reflect: vitality, common strength, willpower, violence, passion, optimism, drive, confidence, carriage, aggression, dominance, and leadership. Fire, or drive, is the catalyst for growth and is associated with spring. All "spring" cards include budding leaves on wands, indicating the first stage of growth.

Cups represent Water: The feminine principle of feeling, nurturing, and intuition. They depict emotional support needed to manifest what we want, psychic ability, receptivity, reflection, passivity, emotion, love, sensitivity, nourishment, sexuality, fertility, children, family life, desire, and psychic ability. Water is a mutable element. Water is a reminder of summer, when seedlings planted in the spring are watered.

Swords represent Air: The masculine principle of thinking and acting. It is ideas in motion, if you like, intellect, reason, swiftness of action, logic, methodology, discrimination, and discernment. The figure is taking an action. The motion and number of swords on a card indicate the type of action it represents. Activity involving a sword is quick. Action that is too rash, without reason, can lead to disastrous consequences.

Pentacles represent Earth: The feminine aspect of life-giving force. In general, they depict manifestation into physical reality, stability of material gain (money flowing in), physical health, work, materialistic gain, home life, the material world. They are attributed to the winter season.

THE COURT CARDS

Each Minor card suit is numbered from 1 to 10, and there are four Royal Cards, or Court Cards: Page, Knight, Queen, and King. Court Card pictures depict a

Figure 3 The Court Cards

single person, their age, status, abilities, qualities, and mental state. Facets of their personalities are mirrored in each suit in relation to the element it corresponds to (see table below). Each deck, therefore, has 16 Court Cards.

When a Court Card occurs in a spread, it may represent a person in the reader's life or the person for whom the reading is given (commonly referred to as the querent) who possesses the card's characteristics. It could also represent the person's qualities that have not been expressed or developed yet.

Pages represent children or young people of either gender, and depict innocence. They represent youthful promise, dreams, and other traits based on the suit, or element, they belong to.

CARD	KEYWORDS	WANDS	CUPS	SWORDS	PENTACLES
KING	Masculine aspect, older man, authority figure, personality, vision, experience	Important, successful, kind, business-minded	Mature, caring, balanced, kind in high position	Powerful, professional, good mind, tough	Financial wizard, wealthy
QUEEN	Feminine aspect, older woman, authority figure, personality, profession, ability	Capable and kind, practical woman. Brunette	Loving, helpful, intuitive	Lonely, mentally able woman, has overcome problems	Abundant, helpful businesswoman. Dark skin/hair
KNIGHT	Young men, movement, action	Business-related travel	Loving, sensitive person	Assertive man, moves quickly	Money-minded, methodical
PAGE	Children, genre, timing	Energetic	Poetic, soft emotional	Bright, difficult	Investment
COMPLEXION	Physical appearance	Strawberry blonde, freckled, brown hair	Fair, light hair/skin	Salt & pepper hair	Dark skin/hair

Figure 4 Court Cards: keywords and meanings

15

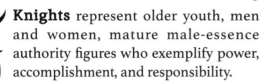

Knights represent older youth, men and women, mature male-essence authority figures who exemplify power, accomplishment, and responsibility.

Queens represent mature maternal figures, usually women who, like kings, wield power. They represent the feminine aspect of wisdom, assurance, fertility, and life-giving abilities.

Kings represent the male aspect, mature authority figures, usually men, who exemplify power, accomplishment, and responsibility.

Tarot Symbology

The Tarot reflects generations of users, as well as other people's thoughts, ideologies, and interpretations that built on the wisdom of past generations; those created their own system of interpretation and imposed it on the Tarot. However, one thing connects all Tarot readers: a desire for a deeper connection with themselves, and more meaningful experiences through seeking guidance.

The Tarot is a compounded symbolic language represented by images, numbers, and a hierarchical structure. When you look at the cards in a spread, all these combinations evoke feelings or senses, allowing you to discover a meaning relevant to you. It may evoke a different meaning for each Tarot reader—that is what the Tarot does. More themes are presented in Chapter Three.

You will notice that the Tarot has a rhythm. This rhythm is represented by the numbering of the cards, the naming of the Major card drawings, the identification of the four elements as the four seasons signifying cycles and timing, and other meanings hidden in each picture. Each season, or cycle, contains cycles within it; there is a process within a process. This makes the Tarot's structure more akin to a matrix of hierarchy, triggering intuition on multiple levels. In many ways, it is like a piece of music. All the components come together to tell a story that evokes sensations that vary from one time to the next, and each person to the other. The hierarchy's rhythm is expressed in the classifications of the Tarot cards as follows:

1. **Major Cards** depict main events or turning points in one's life.

2. **Court Cards** are given higher importance and are represented by Kings, Queens, Knights, and Pages. Their

illustrations and suit depict a single figure in a similar manner to the figures of the Major cards, as well as the characteristics of each figure. They stand a level above the numbered pip cards, although they are not numbered.

3. Minor Cards reflect the cycles and processes of everyday situations.

4. Assigned Ascending Numbers: The ascending numbers on the cards imply a process from beginning to end. Each stage has a meaning or a vibration.

5. The Four Elements Associated with the Four Suits reflect a cycle of seasons, and fluctuating cycles within each season (cards are numbered from 1 to 10).

TAROT CYCLES

The hierarchy of structure in the Tarot cards holds the key to their secrets. It conveys cycles within cycles. The Major cards tell the story of Major cycles of growth and development. Some are upward cycles; others represent inevitable down cycles which are necessary for growth. Minor cycles of the Minor cards, their ascending numbers, and the figures of the Court Cards reflect other, "lesser" cycles of growth and of fluctuating emotional

(cups) and mental (swords) states, as well as attitudes toward achieving goals (wands) and making money (pentacles).

Cause and Effect Cycle

Cycles of life are presented as seasons of the Minor cards' symbols. Each season represents one of the four elements: **Wands** represent growth in spring. **Cups** represent summer, and the water needed to nurture the seeds planted in the spring. **Swords** represent autumn, and the harvest. And finally, **Pentacles**, which represent the element of earth, and winter, represent material gain from selling the harvest.

Seasons are also related to timing. The pip cards' illustrations depict images of real-life situations in each season. When you arrange the pip cards in four rows, one for each season (or element), you will notice that they symbolize actions we all engage in, such as starting creative endeavors, nurturing them, and protecting what we create. They can be hostile at times, but always yield a tangible outcome—whether positive or negative. First, one must initiate action and plant seeds (Wands/spring), then nurture it (Cups/summer) by watering it (supportive emotions), then harvest it (Swords/autumn, shaping the crop), and finally reap the fruits of one's labor (Pentacles/winter, physical reality).

CHAPTER TWO

MEANING OF THE CARDS

The Major and Minor Cards

The Fool is chosen by the Tarot to recount the story and provide the way to self-awareness. He goes through lessons to help him integrate the facets of being a spirit in human form. The Fool finds his place in life at the end of this journey and becomes an integrated individual capable of achieving any goal.

Along the way, he learns how to express himself in a way that is different from how he was raised. Each card teaches him a lesson or points him in the direction of what he must resolve to discover his particular talents, abilities and ways of self-expression. You'll notice parallels between your own life and that of The Fool. The Tarot tale encourages you to reflect on your life while seeking direction to live in a way that is rewarding to you.

The Fool's journey teaches us that not every event is pleasant. Some are difficult, but also necessary for us to grow and establish our own path. His journey teaches us that understanding experiences offers us a fresh perspective, and hence knowledge. It aids in emotional healing, allowing new opportunities to develop.

In effect, we can go through life with joy and ease. To identify his process of self-development, we have divided the Fool's journey into three phases: The Making of a Hero, Inner Alchemy, and Fulfillment.

In the following pages, you will meet the Major and Minor cards as characters and situations that shaped The Fool and helped him integrate his skills, knowledge, self-control, and wisdom. You will encounter different aspects of The Fool in each suit, as the Page, Knight, Queen, and King.

THE MINOR CARDS

Underneath each Major card, the corresponding Minor cards are presented to help you build a more complete picture of the Tarot secrets. For example, the Court Cards represent the developing stages of The Fool's personality: the Pages represent an aspect of The Fool's evolving character. The Knights are an older Fool who becomes The Magician.

The Queens relate to The Empress Card and correspond to developing the feminine aspect of The Fool; and finally, the King Court Cards relate to The Emperor, whom The Fool becomes, having integrated the feminine aspect. Like The Fool, the Court Cards are not numbered.

Moreover, as the Minor cards that follow the Court Cards are numbered, they depict that development in the context of their suit. For example, Wands represent the developmental cycle of The Fool's skills, Cups depict his emotional development, Swords express his evolving thoughts and mastering his mind; and Pentacles express the result of The Fool's developing personality—the culmination of the previous three aspects. In this way, you can begin integrating the meaning of each card, or step of development as it is expressed first as the Major card, then again as the Court Card, and finally as a step, or number of steps, in the daily situations-cycle of the numbered pip cards.

PHASE 1: EXPERIENCING OPPOSITES (CARDS 1–7)

We encounter the characters who helped form and prepare The Fool during his youth in the first phase of the Tarot story. It represents the groundwork that will allow The Fool to make his first decisions on his own, conquer his first conflict, love, and prepare for bigger conflicts. New experiences will aid him in realizing his potential and, ultimately, achieving his life's objective.

0—The Fool: A New Beginning

The Fool's adventure begins with separation or leaving the past behind. He packs his worldly things in a little pouch that he carries on a staff over his shoulder. He wanders carefree under the sun, dressed in bright colors, with a crimson feather in his cap symbolizing his ambitions and a garland of flowers around it. He is about to leap from a cliff. The Fool's faithful companion, the white dog, attempts to warn him by barking at his feet, but The Fool remains unconcerned.

He appears innocent, happy, and full of promise. He is preparing to go on an adventure into the unknown. This trip necessitates understanding the fundamental principles symbolized by the pouch in which he keeps his belongings. His gaze is fixed upward, oblivious to the dangers that await him. Although you might think The Fool is unprepared for this part of his life, the fact that he has chosen to embark on it indicates that he is bold and courageous.

The Fool is also a symbol of everlasting youth and innocence. He holds a white rose in his left hand, symbolizing spiritual longing, and a wand in his right hand, symbolizing the duality of the spiritual and material worlds, respectively. The pouch dangles from the wand's end, containing only the necessities for the voyage—the four elements of air, earth, fire, and water, with which he will learn to realize his aspirations. The Sun is beaming above his head, symbolizing his optimism and faith in life's process.

Moreover, the snow-topped mountains in the distance hint at the challenges he is about to encounter. This contrasts with the shining sun, symbolizing the fluctuating cycle of seasons (bad and fair weather) on the journey.

He isn't foolish, but naive, and it is his innocence and openness to life that keeps him going and provides him with delight. Because he represents every one of us at every stage of our lives, The Fool archetype is profound and significant. Life continues to present new situations in which we feel vulnerable, at risk, and unknown, no matter how old or experienced we are.

The Fool is taking a risk that symbolizes the first step toward self-actualization. Through the experiences he is about to have, he will be transformed. In many respects, he is a juvenile version of an alchemist (The Magician), who begins with simple components and masters them to change his existence into a rewarding experience.

Upright: The card represents sudden opportunities and a decision to embark on an adventure. It expresses the need to let go of old habits and begin something new and unexplored. It denotes someone who is unconventional, courageous, and daring. It can also symbolize meeting someone new, or beginning a new cycle or scenario where you may feel inexperienced or unprepared, depending on where it appears in the spread. The outcome is determined by how effectively you retain your balance. Nonetheless, it is the experience gained from this opportunity that will enrich your life, not the outcome that The Fool represents. Now is the time to think outside the box and believe in yourself and your ability.

Modern Interpretation: Someone with a great deal of potential; a disruptor in a business or field. A young businessperson. A unique and unexpected chance that has the potential to open doors. You'll get an answer if you take a step forward.

Reversed: A hasty decision or connection that could end badly. Before you take the plunge, make sure you've done your homework. Pay attention to your instincts and don't take unnecessary chances.

Court Cards—Pages

The Pages in each Minor card suit represent a younger Fool. They illustrate everyday happenings and the developmental stage of The Fool. Each Court Card suit highlights a different facet of his developing personality.

Meaning: Pages are young people who, depending on the suit to which they belong, reflect youthful potential, dreams, and other characteristics. They encapsulate the tender qualities of a young Fool, which must be nourished for them to mature. Pages are messengers who announce timing and seasons as well as news. In a reading, take note of the Page's corresponding element to get an idea of an event's timing.

Page of Wands is lively, creative, restless or hyperactive, and warm. It also refers to springtime, which is characterized by frenzied activity, new beginnings, inspiration, innovation, and expansion. It tells you to make wise choices in the future, since you will reap what you sow.

Reversed: When this card is reversed in a spread, it denotes a troublesome youngster who has most likely been neglected. They are seeking attention to express their creativity and be acknowledged. As a result, they might behave in an excessive manner. They can be hyperactive and lack concentration.

Page of Cups represents a child's imaginative, emotional, and poetic character. The Page of Cups is a sensitive, sympathetic individual who is easily hurt. When it occurs in a spread, the card encourages you to develop your creative side rather than being lazy or daydreaming! It's a call to action to make your dreams a reality right now.

Reversed: An overly emotional youngster—or the reader's current state.

Page of Swords is a bright, athletic but possibly difficult young person. They are witty and intelligent. Their actions may be hasty, but they are intellectually curious and fast to pick up new information. They have the potential to be introverted. This is a child who appreciates sports and active games. This card also represents polishing one's abilities and skills to advance in life.

Reversed: Indicates a significant mental state, or the need for professional assistance to address one's mental state.

Page of Pentacles: This card represents a young person who is studious or financially savvy. If you've just started a project, it could also mean profit or minor winnings. This is a youth who is inquisitive and has financial intelligence.

Reversed: A child, or someone who acts childishly and has personality issues because of their serious nature. Interacting with others is tough for them.

1—The Magician: The Initiator

The card describes The Fool's first lesson. Early in his journey, he learns that no matter what his goals are, he has a natural potential to enhance his abilities, skills, and talents. These he must cultivate to achieve his goals. The Fool must learn to channel his creative force into the tools and equipment represented by the four elements on the magician's table. We see The Fool transforming into a skilled "magician" who masters his inner resources and abilities.

Essentially, to fulfill his goals and get results, The Magician taps into universal powers, bridging his inner resources with the universal or spiritual power of inspiration. The Fool has matured into The Magician, who realizes that he must maintain balance by reconciling Spirit and materialism. By seeking inspiration and gaining techniques to actualize goals, he represents both the feminine and masculine principles. The Magician exhibits this by raising one arm to the skies and holding a white wand that represents purity of intention and spiritual awareness, while pointing down to the Earth with the other hand, which represents logic, practicality, and earthy skills.

However, for his aspirations and ideas to come true, he must retain a sense of balance—but first, he must act. In front of The Magician, the four elements of creation are represented by a cup (water), a pentacle or a desk (earth), a wand (fire), and a sword (air). These qualities must be developed and mastered to express his talents and achieve his goals. As the four elements suggest, there is a cycle for growth. Emotions, thoughts, and actions must be oriented toward that goal in order for it to become real. The Magician's red robe and white garment underneath symbolize his pure intention, his focused mind, and his will to see his intentions through to completion—and he develops a plan to do so. This card represents the limitless possibilities we are born with, as well as the necessity to learn new abilities and hone our inner resources to achieve our goals.

The Magician is unafraid of risks. He knows what he wants to achieve, and why. He does not hesitate, because he is aware of his circumstance. He can concentrate with a single-mindedness. He remains the perfect conduit for miracles if he remembers the heavenly source of his power. In a reading, The Magician suggests that you have access to the fundamental forces of creativity if you can claim your power and act with awareness and concentration. This card is a call to action: act now if you know what you want and are determined to achieve it.

Upright: The Magician card represents the use of reasoning or methodology to achieve one's goals. If you are upright, you have willpower, a strong intellect, initiative, flexibility, and physical/mental focus. The Magician predicts that you will complete your plans and that your project will take off. This card represents a writer with a creative touch, a sharp, creative, business-oriented person, and a future leader.

Modern Representation: The Magician represents a creative person, someone with a good balance of logical and creative qualities, who speaks well and expresses their ideas clearly.

Reversed: Confusion, loss of concentration, worry, and failure to carry ideas to an acceptable finish are all signs of learning difficulties. Plans that were once good are being abandoned. Revisit your goal and take steps to achieve it; create a strategy and a procedure, then hone the abilities you'll need to make it a reality.

Court Cards—The Knights

The Knights represent a stage in The Fool's development from a Page to a Magician, and then to a King (or Queen.) They represent energy and action, and symbolize the creative, emotional, mental, and tangible results The Fool achieves as the four aspects of his personality evolve. In a reading, they represent youths, older than Pages, who are on the lookout for ways to express themselves by identifying their innate strengths and capabilities.

Knight of Wands: This Knight depicts a young man galloping across the desert, symbolizing the promise of expansion (from a desert to a garden or forest). Over his suit of armor he wears a cape embroidered with salamanders. He exudes purpose and assurance as he holds the reins of the horse in one hand, suggesting confidence, and a wand in the other, symbolizing creative force and drive. The young man has brilliant ideas and a sense of adventure; he is a generous and warm friend or lover, yet he can be impulsive, inconsistent, and hasty in his decisions. He has a terrific sense of humor and will go to any length to have a good time. This knight may also indicate foreign business connections.

Upright: This card represents an occasion or event, a change of location, a long journey, or even immigration to a new country.

Reversed: Business activities not going as planned, not very helpful, causes problems, project muddled, unfinished.

Knight of Cups: Soft, sensitive, poetic, creative, dreamer. This card depicts an artistic, caring, and amorous young man. Unlike the confident gallop of the Knight of Wands, his white horse bows coyly and moves gently and deliberately. His spiritual goals are symbolized by his winged helmet. And his clothes are embellished with the fish of creative imagination. A stream crosses the terrain in the background, implying the line that separates conscious and unconscious sentiments. He represents a sophisticated, highly principled youth, an idealist, and a seeker of perfection and emotional truth.

Upright: This card usually denotes a marriage proposal, a project in the realm of art, or a love arrival. It signifies an arousing

caution when it appears in a spread. While you may admire the romanticism, be careful not to be led astray by this romantic type.

Reversed: Unfaithful, led astray, emotional problems.

Knight of Swords: Consider the way this Knight is rendered in comparison to the previous ones. Notice the horse and the scene's background. The Knight of Swords appears to be racing across the card, leaning forward in his saddle, sword drawn and ready to attack. Notice how the horse's legs are extended, and how its mane is blowing in the wind. Both images convey movement and quick action. In the corner, you will see the cypress trees in the background, which represent grief or hardship; these have been bent by the force of the wind.

The Knight of Swords is an odd mix: a fascinating personality that draws others' attention and affection. However, he has a ruthless streak, and while he is not malicious, he tends to harm others in pursuit of his ambitions. He doesn't offer emotional support; he doesn't think about it. He does, however, possess a sharp mind and a strong business sense, and he excels in his field.

25

Upright: This is an assertive young person who moves quickly and makes their presence felt. Enthusiastic. As a situation, he may represent an event that begins with a flurry of excitement and then fades almost as fast as it began, leaving chaos in its wake.

Reversed: Troublemaker, deceitful, can be violent (if card appears in a spread with The Tower + The Devil). Argumentative.

Knight of Pentacles: The Knight of Pentacles differs from the other three Knights in a significant way. His horse is pictured patiently studying the surroundings in a recently plowed field (results are emerging). The image is serene. This Knight possesses boundless patience and tolerance! Furthermore, he is trustworthy, and will complete a task no matter how long it takes. He never fails to achieve his objectives because he never gives up. Others seek out his attributes of endurance and the capacity for honest effort.

Upright: This is a finance-oriented, analytical, slow-moving young man, someone who is methodical, reliable, and logical. This person is sensible, systematic, and stable in his approach, and he can be trusted. In a spread, he signifies a happy outcome of a situation, particularly business ventures that have gone on for a long time or appeared unfruitful at first.

Reversed: Represents someone who cannot be trusted with money, is too focused on it, or has financial/career troubles.

Minor Cards—The Aces

The Ace, or number 1, represents the start of everything. One is the number of creative potential and power. It is the starting point from which all other numbers develop. Aces show a tremendous burst of energy. They represent new beginnings that are essential, positive, and forceful. Ace cards depict a hand appearing from the clouds hanging over the element of the suit. This may suggest that manifestation of all things arises from one aspect: an idea or a thought, since clouds represent the air element, leading up to The Ace of Pentacles, which denotes the beginning of realizing tangible, physical results—the end of the four-season cycle of The Fool creating his own reality.

Ace of Wands: Growth of New Ideas

The image on the card is of a hand clutching a budding wand as it emerges from a cloud. A castle on a hill in the distance represents the goal, and what the future may hold. Wands correspond to fire, creativity, inventiveness, and vitality. The Ace of Wands denotes a fresh start and new ideas or projects. Aces symbolize energy in its purest form. The Ace of Wands thus expresses pure creativity.

Upright: This card can represent a new commercial enterprise, a fresh endeavor, a new foundation and creative ability—all of which have a lot of promise and aspiration to succeed.

Reversed: Projects and ideas encounter creative stumbling blocks or delays. Things are not likely to get off the ground right now.

Ace of Cups: New Strong Emotional Connections

The Ace of Cups shows a hand emerging from a cloud, suggesting an opportunity that appears out of nowhere. The five senses are represented by five streams of water that spring from the cup and descend into a pond of lilies. The water lily is a metaphor for emotional development. Spiritual principles are symbolized by the dove diving into the cup. The cups are associated with water, the element that governs feelings and emotions. As a result, the purest part of emotional energy is represented by the Ace of Cups.

Upright: It denotes the start of a new relationship, the reawakening of strong emotions, love, marriage, motherhood, and great joy or satisfaction derived from a loving partnership. If The Lovers card appears in the same spread as The Hierophant or Justice, it implies a marriage proposal.

Reversed: Emotional turmoil. Happiness isn't long-lasting, and love's energy is dwindling.

Ace of Swords: Inevitable Powerful Change (for the better)

The two-edged sword on the Ace of Swords indicates that it can cut both ways. It is a card of enormous force and strength. All thoughts and actions have either a positive or a negative consequence. The crown on the sword is a symbol of attainment. Two leaves hang from the crown; on the right is a palm leaf, representing victory, and on the left is an olive branch, symbolizing peace. Either victory or peace can be attained by the sword. This suit is associated with the element of air, and is symbolic of the intellect, reason, or strategic thinking. The Ace of Swords is a card of perseverance in the face of hardship, and it frequently signifies that something good will emerge

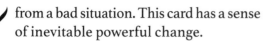

from a bad situation. This card has a sense of inevitable powerful change.

Upright: Signifies strong forces at play, which may herald problems. However, the message of this card is also that you have the ability to overcome obstacles; the right mind-set is essential. It's a time for making decisions and moving in a new direction.

Reversed: A phase or cycle of tension.

Ace of Pentacles: Receiving a Large Sum of Money

In this card, a golden pentacle is offered by the hand coming out of the cloud, denoting positive results for hard work. This is mirrored by the image of a well-kept garden underneath the pentacle. The Pentacles represent the earth element, which represents the body, matter, and material achievements. The Ace of Pentacles indicates a successful start and financial security. It can also refer to a lump-sum payment received unexpectedly as gift or a bonus, as opposed to borrowing money.

Upright: The Ace of Pentacles represents a fresh opportunity or venture that you must seize and put your skills to use; or receiving a large sum of money.

Reversed: Indicates a difficulty with the tangible world. Smaller sums of money are received.

2—The High Priestess: The Unseen/ Intuition

The Magician may have imagination, a process, and logic; what he lacks is intuition, which is represented by The High Priestess. Here The Fool (now The Magician) is faced with the unknown. He must learn to acknowledge and develop his psychic instinct. The High Priestess sits on a throne between two white and black columns, symbolizing nature's duality: positive and negative forces, the conscious and unconscious, the essence and the not-yet-manifest form, darkness and light, and the dual nature of the feminine—birth-giving or destructive. A veil decorated with pomegranates (representing fertility) hangs between the pillars, through which water may be seen, flowing toward a crescent moon lying at her feet.

She sits passively in plain blue robes, hands clasped gently, holding a scroll with the inscription Torah, the law of natural wisdom. Her ethereal aspect contrasts with The Empress' earthly wealth and fertility. Yet the two combined form the feminine principle, or the nature of spiritual and earthly mother. Too much emphasis on one leads to an imbalance.

The treasures of the unconscious mind are brought to consciousness through The High Priestess. She can also signify a link to the occult and the esoteric, as well as heightened hearing or mediumship. The unseen or unknown alludes to hidden talents and potential that must be revealed. All life began in darkness: the blackness of the womb or the darkness of the soil. As a result, a period of gestation is required for the formation and birth of a new life.

The waxing and waning **Moon** is represented by the silver crown on her head, with the full orb in the center. Her blue-and-white cloak cascades to the ground, resembling a torrent of water. The water behind the curtain represents treasures hidden in the unconscious mind, as well as the changing lunar cycles and emotional sensitivity guided by the phases of the Moon. She wears a solar cross on her breast to symbolize the union of male and female duality, the hidden and the revealed.

Upright: The spiritual celestial mother and heightened feminine perceptive nature. In a spread, it means that something is about to be disclosed. It also represents unconscious beliefs, fears, or emotions, as well as the ability to seek advice through dreams. It represents psychic abilities as well as a curiosity in mystical and esoteric studies, and the development of feminine abilities of intuition. This card urges you to explore your unconscious, and the meaning of your dreams. As an outcome card, it indicates that the future is undetermined; be patient. It can also signify a pregnant woman, depending on where it occurs in a spread.

Modern Interpretation: A sensitive artist, channeler, musician, medium, healer, or mental healer. A diplomat or peacemaker, they enjoy a higher sense of perception and gentleness, and can perceive the wants and needs of others. Also, it represents someone who makes an excellent counselor.

Reversed: Negative psychic influences, self-delusion. Using psychic abilities to manipulate; drug and alcohol overuse. In a reversed position, The High Priestess might suggest mental illness, a muddled mind, and suppressed or neglected intuitive feelings, as it relates to clairaudient and clairvoyant aptitude. It can represent hidden influences, someone who is working against you, or that you are surrounded by shallow, superficial individuals, depending on where it appears in a spread. This card warns you to be cautious, and to keep your own counsel.

The Minor Cards—The Twos

Positive and negative, male and female, spirit and matter, ego and higher purpose, conscious and subconscious and so on are examples of complementary opposites represented by 2. To achieve balance and harmony, The Ace's pure energy is split into two opposing forces. The duality of the twos is expressed in the Minor cards that follow in each suit. It might signify either a balance of forces or unrealized creativity.

Two of Wands: A Choice of a Collaborative Partnership

Wands signify ambition and initiative. The man in the image stands atop the castle's foundations, his wands firmly planted on the ground, indicating everything he has accomplished. He has a small globe in one hand that shows expansion possibilities. He seems to be deliberating his next move. The pattern on his castle battlements, white lilies, signify pure thought, while red roses reflect desire and ambition. The card's essence is potential that is yet to be realized, even though the combination implies a well-balanced disposition.

Upright: This card suggests a new outlook on a situation, high ambitions and goals, a desire to travel, or foreign connections. It denotes success as well as expansion based on strength and vision. Taking initiative can help you overcome obstacles.

Reversed: There are issues with your partnership, or it is not working.

Two of Cups: Love Affair, Relationship Development, Good Friendship

In this card, the number 2 is symbolized by a balance of two opposites: a man and a woman swapping cups. The cups represent love and emotion as well as the pure energy that emanates from The Ace of Cups, which is now divided between two people. Both of their interests and intentions must be considered. This marriage of opposites, symbolized by the intertwined snakes, reflects spiritual and physical love, and brings healing and support.

Upright: This card represents the start of a good and balanced relationship or friendship. The spouses share their sentiments and create a balanced environment based on harmony and cooperation. It symbolizes the emotional balance needed in order to achieve goals. It denotes a commitment or engagement, a marriage proposal, or the resolution of a fight or dispute.

Reversed: Separation, or an emotional imbalance in the relationship.

Two of Swords: Strained Situation, a Decision Is Required Between Two Alternatives

The blindfolded seated woman in the Two of Swords represents a stalemate in which the figure is unable to see a way out. She appears to be holding both blades in balance, but the future is uncertain. She's sitting on the edge of the water, oblivious to the breaking waves (her emotions) against the rocks (the hard reality of her predicament) behind her. It represents the necessity for courage to overcome a state of fear. This impasse will be broken by confronting the facts and deciding.

Upright: This card resembles the image of blind justice, which implies that the current situation is the outcome of previous deeds. A judgment or choice can be made based on the facts, and the situation can be overcome.

Reversed: Outbursts of emotion, losing one's temper, arguing without thinking first.

Two of Pentacles: Balanced Finances, Beneficial Partnerships, Collaboration

A young man "juggling" or balancing two pentacles symbolizes the expression of the number 2 in this suit. Despite the strong seas in the background, he appears playful. This shows how adaptability and open-mindedness can lead to a solution, perhaps a new means of generating money. To keep abundance flowing, you must create and balance both streams of income. In other words, success is the result of deft manipulation. A harmonious transition in financial affairs is predicted, especially if the individual is adaptable.

Upright: This card's message implies that you can develop two streams of income to help you balance your finances. Go for it!

Reversed: Financial issues, or the inability to balance your finances.

3—The Empress: Growth and Abundance

The Empress is a representation of the fertile, life-giving mother who rules over nature's bounty and the Earth's rhythms. All the delights and joys of the senses, as well as a profusion of new life in all its forms, flow from her. The Empress encourages you to develop your connection to nature—the source of our existence.

A garden and forest serve as The Empress' backdrop. She is a representation of abundance. She wears large, colorful robes hinting at pregnancy or what is yet to come. This implies that a promise has been realized—the realization of consistent effort. The pomegranate represents conjugal love, while the sheaf of corn represents fertility. The 12 stars on her crown signify the 12 months of the year and the 12 zodiac signs. Infinite cycles of time are made finite and represent the 12 hours of the day and night. The Empress symbolizes the natural rhythm of the cycles or seasons of life: from seed to flower, fruit and, finally, decay. The water pouring into a pool in front of her represents male and female merging to produce and nurture new life, while the forest represents abundance, depicting growth cycles throughout the year. The astrological sign of Venus, ruler of Taurus, the sign linked with nature, is shown on the heart-shaped shield by her feet.

Moreover, The Fool learns about women, their nature, and how to care for and nurture bodily needs from his earthly mother, The Empress. He learns about natural growth as well as the cycles of death and rebirth, and the cycles that men and women go through in their relationships.

The Empress is a symbol of happiness and stability in partnerships. Her enigmatic smile represents the realization of one's potential in all forms of abundance: love, marriage, and motherhood.

In a reading, The Empress can represent any nurturing aspect of motherhood. As a Major Arcana card, her qualities transcend motherhood to its essence, which is the giving of life (to ideas, projects, or business as well as children) and nurturing it. In a reading, The Empress suggests financial reward, but only until you understand that wealth comes with a generous, open heart.

Upright: This card represents timing, the changing rhythm of nature, and taking the right action at the right time to realize ideas, nurture them, and reap the fruits of consistent efforts to sustain them. It is a positive card that denotes abundant living and caring for one's physical health to fulfill one's mission. In a spread, it can indicate a pregnancy, birth, happiness around an occasion or an event, fulfillment, fertility, pleasure, love affairs, and marriages. If the card falls in the house of career, it denotes a business or product connected with women. In a reading, it represents a warm, loving, sensual person with a nurturing nature.

Modern Interpretation: Successful female-centered business, art dealer, event organizer, wedding planner, content creator, nurturing mentor.

Reversed: Overindulgence in pleasure and material things. Sterility or miscarriage (of ideas or children), the end of a love affair, inharmonious influence. Blocked creativity, material discomfort, sex without love, a pleasure-seeking nature, an unwanted child, or an abortion.

Court Cards—The Queens

Queens represent older authoritative women, symbolizing their personality or profession. They denote the feminine creative aspect of one's personality. Queens and Kings do not tend to represent timing of events. In a spread, they depict personalities. Generally, they are depicted as noble-looking women sitting on a throne, reflecting their authority and abilities.

Queen of Wands: The throne of the Queen of Wands is adorned with flaming lion motifs. She wields a wand in one hand and a sunflower in the other, symbolizing her strength and power. The black cat sits at her feet, symbolizing the Queen's status as the creator of her life at home. She can successfully run a house and a family while still finding energy and motivation to pursue her own passions and aspirations. She is loved by those around her and helps her friends without getting distracted from what she values most. However, if she is ever crossed, she fights back fiercely, like a lioness! Her unwavering adaptability is a desirable trait.

Upright: Capable entrepreneur. She is an enabler, and a kind and practical woman.

Reversed: She can be forceful if crossed.

Queen of Cups: The Queen of Cups is a dreamy woman who sits on a throne adorned with baby mermaids. As she gazes into an elaborate cup with handles shaped like angels' wings, her flowing clothing mingles with the pool of water at her feet. The cup she is holding has a lid, suggesting that she is aware of feelings—even unconscious ones. Known as the Queen of Emotions (or hearts), she has attained a deep understanding of her own emotions as well as those of others.

Upright: Artistic and intuitive; a loving, helpful, intuitive woman (fair in complexion).

Reversed: Woman of dreamy nature, disconnected from reality. Someone who gives more than they receive and suffers for sacrificing their own emotional needs.

Queen of Swords: The Queen of Swords has a solemn demeanor. Her throne is adorned with butterflies and an angel. In the background, notice the storm clouds and the darkening sky. Her cloak is decorated with clouds representing her pensive nature and mental acumen, symbolized by holding the sword. Her straight sword and stern face show her determination. She depicts a woman who has suffered loss and may be alone; she could be a widow, divorced, or separated. She has loved and lost, but she knows the cycles of life. For now, she must wait, but she knows she will find love again. She faces her pain patiently and courageously, like a queen. The Queen of Swords represents a strong-willed woman who can cope with whatever life throws at her, and make the best of it.

Upright: Lonely; a mentally capable woman who overcomes obstacles.

Reversed: A person who is not facing the reality of their situation. Overcome with grief or feeling sorry for herself, she can be cruel and selfish. Can indicate muddled thinking and a narrow or limited perspective.

Queen of Pentacles: The Queen of Pentacles sits contentedly on her throne, surrounded by a lush, fertile background. Flowers and rabbits, which represent fertility, are framed on the card. She is a pragmatic woman who appreciates material possessions and is skilled at obtaining them, since she appears to be enjoying herself. She understands what she wants and is happy when she gets it. She also accepts responsibility for her judgments, and is fair and wise in business; she is affluent due to her hard work. She represents a helpful friend or employer with a generous personality and the ability to provide realistic advice.

Upright: This card describes a well-off, realistic, and supportive woman; she may be a businessperson. The Queen of Coins would make an excellent adviser or mentor. She is supportive, practical, and wealthy.

Reversed: A materialistic, selfish personality, someone who takes more than they give. Moreover, someone who is unable to manage their finances or business and is heading toward failure or bankruptcy.

Minor Cards—The Threes
The number 3 represents The Empress as well as progress and expansion. The

number 2 represents the two partners who collaborate (on a proposal or a project); the number 3 sees the collaboration through to completion. It represents the achievement of the first phase.

Three of Wands: The man who featured in The Two of Wands reappears here. This time he is looking over a much larger horizon. This is symbolized by the three Wands he had planted in the ground. The decision he made after contemplating in The Two of Wands has taken him to the next set. His consistent efforts have been rewarded. He is ready to move beyond what he has achieved. The card's message is this: the person who works relentlessly toward his objective will cross the finish line—and beyond. Moreover, the next phase of growth will come quickly.

Upright: Success and expansion. This card indicates that although much has been achieved, there is more success and expansion to come. Rejoice!

Modern Interpretation: Expansion of business through more branches, franchising, overseas branches, or international growth.

Reversed: One has lost an opportunity or missed out on a collaboration that could have led to growth and success.

Three of Cups: In a cheerful celebration, three maidens dance while each carries her cup. This indicates a celebration shared by a group. Flowers and fruits are plentiful around the feet, indicating the extent of the celebration and reaping the fruits or rewards of the happy union or collaboration of The Two of Cups. This card can represent a marriage or a birth as well as emotional growth, happiness, and accomplishments. It also denotes recovery from emotional wounds. Although it is a wonderful and exciting moment, like with The Three of Wands, it is merely the beginning.

Upright: Celebration. Birth of a child. The success of a new business or joint venture.

Reversed: Lost opportunity or pregnancy, or an occasion celebrated too soon.

Three of Swords: The background is gloomy, indicating stormy weather ahead. Together, the heart and the swords indicate emotional and mental turmoil. As a result of this disappointment, there may be quarrels or separations. However, as swift as the swords are, a flash of insight might occur, allowing the person to put this sorrow into perspective and begin to heal. Even though this is a sad time, there is a sense of clearing the ground or the beginning of something new. Swords are symbolic of a person's thinking and perception, and therefore imply that challenges in a relationship, or a degree of disappointment and sorrow, can be overcome if confronted with honesty.

Upright: Emotional quarrels and separation. Love affair ends due to one of the partners being unfaithful.

Reversed: The person is hanging onto the sorrow without facing the facts of the situation or deciding to move on and get a new perspective on it. An end leads to a new beginning.

Three of Pentacles: Three people, or craftsmen, are depicted in this image; they appear to be discussing plans. This implies that one stage has been achieved, and plans for the next phase are being made. Furthermore, it signifies that the foundation of the project or business was a solid one, and that material gain was achieved because of the efforts made.

Upright: Commercial collaboration, outcome, and planning. Abilities and talents that will help you succeed. Joint collaborations with others will be a success. Financial affairs will prosper. Also, skills you already have can lead to a successful business if you apply them.

Reversed: Problems with a project, delayed success, or unnecessary anxiety over business. A break is needed to maintain balance. It can also indicate sudden opportunities and the need to develop (more) skills to achieve success. Finances are currently blocked—activate your skills to create money flow. The help of collaborators needs to be acknowledged.

4—The Emperor: Authority and Structure

The Emperor represents The Empress' masculine side. As The Fool's earthly father, he is the complementary role model to The Empress. The Fool learns about authority, reason, power, and structure from him. After learning about The Empress' yielding, intuitive, and giving nature, The Fool now learns about balancing it with structure and leadership aspects.

The Emperor signifies material stability and big, worldly achievements that necessitate focus, hard work, and dedication. It also indicates the difficulty of adhering to principles and making a commitment.

The message of this card is: things do not come easily, but they will surely happen.

The Fool leaves behind the natural, nurturing softness of The Empress to learn from his earthly father. The challenge is striking a balance between worldly desires and what is important in the long run. The Emperor strives to build long-lasting structures—a legacy. Notice that his throne is made of solid, gray, and everlasting stone, the opposite of the luscious and colorful throne of The Empress. His red robes signify his drive and determination. He appears stern in adhering to his commitments. He knows that higher ambitions take time to be realized, and that building a solid foundation is essential. The Emperor is the essence of leadership in devising plans, structure, methodology, overseeing the implementation of ideas to the end, and holding people accountable.

Note The Emperor's armor, disguised by his red cloak. It implies his inner constitution and power that lie beneath enormous strength. The jewels on his head signify his financial prosperity and rank, while the orb he holds symbolizes his rational grasp of the laws that must be followed by humans. The scepter is a symbol of masculine power and inventiveness. The image conveys a strong sense of authority, power, and prosperity. The Emperor instructs The Fool on matters of authority, leadership, administration, rules, and moral and ethical behavior. The Emperor's posture is strikingly close to that of Justice, which embodies similar traits; the balance of justice must be upheld.

The Emperor's essence is a representation of spiritual creative forces channeled into dynamic force, creating solid and functioning ideas. He represents the desire for ambition, power, riches, and fame. In contrast to his consort, The Empress, whose feminine energy is receptive and caring, he communicates in a straightforward and strong manner. The Empress and The Emperor's connections offer the complete and crucial lesson to The Fool about the dual nature of each person. An excess of either masculine or feminine attributes can be damaging. An equation involving opposites needs to be balanced. While The Emperor strives for perfection, The Empress is content with the best that can be achieved within the constraints of earthly reality. Both elements of The Emperor and Empress are necessary; without them, harmony and balance cannot be achieved. Nevertheless, it is important to recognize when compromise is necessary.

Upright: Represents structure, power, and wisdom. A man with authority who can build stability and has achieved worldly success. It also represents dealing with an authority figure, like a boss, or someone who is their own boss. Can symbolize a man who has difficulty expressing emotion or is unwilling to let his defenses down (note the other cards in the spread).

Modern Interpretation: CEO, architect, just leader; someone who works in the armed forces, or a politician.

Reversed: Immature, selfish, domineering. Hatred of authority or about to lose authority. Feeling threatened, drained, vulnerable, lacking in ambition. Overshadowed by a dominant parent. A man who is exploiting his authority by acting foolishly. The latter can also be advice to the seeker, depending on the purpose of the spread.

Court Cards—The Kings

Kings are the male counterparts of Queens, and in readings represent men. They, like Queens, represent authority. You might notice that the Queens appear relaxed on their throne, while the Kings are poised for action with respect to their suits. These archetypes are an invitation to integrate both aspects harmoniously.

King of Wands: This is a vivid image of a king, whose clock and background are decorated with lions and curled salamanders. A real salamander stands alongside him, preparing for action as well. The salamander's sinuous body, and its ability to bend and twist with ease, suggests not only the element of fire but also charm and sexual appeal that can be magnetic. Its wet skin reminds us that fire frequently needs the element of water to cool down!

The King has wit and charm. He is friendly and generous, with a wonderful sense of humor and a desire to have a good time. Because he is entertaining and upbeat, he can persuade anyone to do anything. He never runs out of fresh ideas or insights, and he is ready to decide on difficult matters whenever they arise. However, he can overlook minor details and become agitated, or lose his optimism when met with the reality of details. He follows his instincts and is unfazed by setbacks.

Upright: Successful entrepreneur. Important, kind, interested in business.

Reversed: Represents an impractical person who might overvalue their looks or charm in the face or practical achievement. In other words, promises a great deal, but without tangible results.

King of Cups: The King of Cups, on the other hand, sits atop a throne, seemingly uneasy, as he overlooks stormy seas. A fish leaps over the waves in the distance but he is oblivious to it. The golden fish around his neck represents his imagination. It seems to be a hollow token compared to the vibrant imagination behind him. His feet do not touch the water, implying that he wants to connect with his unconscious emotions—unlike his Queen, who blends into the waves. Despite being the master of emotions, his mood swings (symbolized by the stormy water under his throne) imply that he is not fully connected to his element, that he is troubled by expressing his emotions and feelings, or is duty-bound to make others happy. Masculinity is generally associated with conscious cognition and intellect. However, this King seems uncomfortable in the world of emotions. Rather than express his feelings, he tends to pay lip service to them. If the King of Cups appears in a spread, it represents an aspect of the private personality behind the image. It indicates that the man concerned is having difficulty connecting with his feelings.

Upright: Balanced and caring. Mature, kind, and in a high position.

Reversed: The person concerned may be a romantic, charming talker; often his words are hollow, without genuine feeling. It represents an unreliable, unfaithful, two-faced man.

King of Swords: The King of Swords looks calmly, straight ahead, wearing a purple cloak symbolizing wisdom, while he holds his sword upright, unfazed by the stormy clouds building up—a common sight in the suit of Swords. The air appears to be still; we see the cypress trees standing erect. This King exudes strength, self-assurance, and conviction. The Sword represents the mind and the air element; it emphasizes a desire for truth and justice. Can you find the parallels between this card and a Justice card? A plea for forgiveness or compassion will not influence The King of Swords. He tends to be suspicious and over-cautious, on the negative side. However, his sense of justice and fairness are admirable as long as they can be modified with compassion.

Upright: Older man with an authoritative personality, vision, and experience. Someone who gives truthful advice or fair opinions, although they may seem harsh.

Reversed: A manipulative, uncompassionate or mentally violent man or boss.

King of Pentacles: The King of Pentacles, like The Empress figure or his counterpart, The Queen of Pentacles, is surrounded by wealth and fruits of the earth. His throne is adorned with a bull's head, symbolizing the earth sign of Taurus—the love of material possessions, maintaining a warm and nurturing home life. He is depicted casually resting his hand over the pentacle, whereas most figures in this suit hold the pentacle underneath. This indicates that he has mastered his physical reality with confidence and is therefore not obsessed with material gain. Notice the majestic castle behind him, which symbolizes his earthly achievements.

He is a man who adores money and is content to amass and enjoy it. He's a bit of a financial whiz when it comes to business. He is not, however, corrupt. Quite the opposite—he is patient and earns money the hard way, through ethical business practices. He is generous, and shares the results of his labor with others. This card's message, or the lesson he offers The Fool, is to be satisfied with what you have. Enjoy your wealth, but remember that as much as you cherish it, you need to work hard for it.

Upright: Financial wizard, wealthy. Financial security. Honest. It refers to an older, mature man on whom you can rely. He is compassionate, self-made, and extremely successful in business. He is helpful, but he has high standards for others.

Reversed: An unethical person who can be thrifty and overly possessive.

Minor Cards—The Fours

A square with equal sides is represented by the number 4: reality, logic, reason, and structure. It is also man's threefold nature—mind, body, and spirit—that is brought to the material plane, making a square that symbolizes "stable manifestation," having understood the law of Spirit.

Four of Wands: The two central characters in the background, carrying bouquets high over their heads, herald news of a celebration. It also reflects that it is time to rest and enjoy the fruits of one's labor (or take a vacation). The bridge over the moat and the castle behind it represent success, and the act of crossing the bridge to get to your destination. The garland that adorns the four wands in the foreground represents the success that is about to be celebrated. If you look closely, you will notice a mix of fruits, flowers, and lilies that represent the fruits of labor while upholding spiritual values. The Four of Wands represents the characteristics of the Wands, which result in productivity and contentment.

Upright: Enjoyable collaboration, a restful break, or a vacation.

Reversed: Problems with a project or business. Delayed success, or unnecessary anxiety over business or work. A rest is needed. The end of a career, or forced change.

Four of Cups: A young man sits cross-legged with his arms folded because of the turbulent emotions overwhelming him. He seems unhappy, looking at three cups in front of him while ignoring or denying a fourth cup offered by a hand emerging from the cloud. He looks conflicted. The steadiness represented in number 4 is not embodied. This is because an important component is missing: an understanding of the situation's wisdom. This card represents a call to examine circumstances.

Upright: Boredom. Re-evaluating emotional affairs or connections. Indulging in an emotional state and ignoring opportunities.

Reversed: Lack of enthusiasm, fear of being alone, or indulging in disappointment to the extent that one is missing new, unexpected opportunities.

Four of Swords: This image depicts the effigy of a Knight resting over his tomb. Although it seems threatening, because three swords are hanging over him and a fourth is fixed to his tomb, it denotes a much-needed rest after a long and tiring struggle. It indicates healing and convalescence to gather energy and recharge. The three swords hanging over him are not touching him, perhaps indicating that he is too worried about the need to fight; but the fourth sword, underneath him, indicates that it's time to rest. Notice the stained-glass window in the top left corner, depicting an angel or saint with a halo around its head, blessing the kneeling figure. The halo seems to spell out PAX—"peace" in Latin. The message of this card is that getting control over our thoughts and worries brings peace.

Upright: Rest is needed. Stop worrying!

Reversed: Enforced rest, feeling alone.

Four of Pentacles: In this image, a man is seen clutching the gold he has earned.

Another gold coin hangs over the crown on his head, indicating thoughts of future monetary gain. This card represents both the number 4's strength of purpose and the pentacle's monetary aspect. "Save half of what you make while investing the other half wisely" is the card's message.

Upright: Doing well financially. Financial matters are your top priority, and you are well positioned to excel in that area. Remember to set aside money for savings as well as some to reinvest in your business.

Reversed: A spendthrift or miser.

5—The Hierophant: Versatility and Freedom

The Fool learns about accepting his intuitive nature and maintaining a connection to higher wisdom by acknowledging his sense of knowing. He upholds his values and moral responsibilities. The Hierophant, or pope, is the carrier and transmitter of spirituality and wisdom. He represents an "evolved" mind.

The celestial, or spiritual, parents are The Hierophant and his counterpart, The High Priestess. By learning from both, The Fool's personality is integrated. His connection to Spirit is encouraged through developing his knowing and intuition. He is encouraged to find a higher purpose—his destiny. While The High Priestess represents hidden knowledge, or the ethereal world, The Fool must obtain the revealed knowledge and wisdom of The Hierophant to fulfill his earthly desires.

Between the celestial parents, The Fool's personality is balanced, integrating the feminine, receptive side with the masculine, action side. On another level, The Hierophant symbolizes the wisdom of connecting with a higher spiritual purpose that is behind materialistic human ambitions, and a deep sense of knowing since all secret knowledge was revealed to him. The Fool's ability to maintain the flow of abundance, while realizing his destiny by touching the lives of others, is due to integrating the two: hidden and revealed knowledge.

Although religious in essence, this image serves as a symbol for all types of initiations (note the two figures in front of The Hierophant, and his hand raised toward them). Youngsters in any culture are taught to abide by society's customs and adopt a certain worldview. The Hierophant represents all structures within a society, such as schools, clubs, teams, and companies. Moreover, this card symbolizes The Hierophant initiating The Fool to find his own way, his own expression, and follow his destiny.

Upright: Conventional learning as well as intuitive knowing. Spiritual marriage ceremony when coupled with The Lovers card and Justice. It also denotes a gifted "teacher," an old friend, or an older person who gives sound advice. The Hierophant symbolizes a high level of consciousness, a natural teacher or counselor. It describes a person who has knowledge and wisdom, and applies it to make his vision a reality. In a spread, this card indicates that one's destiny is about to be fulfilled.

Modern Interpretation: Lateral thinker. Inspirational speaker, a person in the diplomatic corps, a mediator or charismatic actor. Someone with high moral standards.

Reversed: Materialistic. Unorthodox. Rebellion against the establishment. If seeking advice from an accountant or lawyer, get a second opinion. Do not rush into new agreements. They might prove disappointing!

The Minor Cards—The Fives

Five represents flexibility and openness, the opposite of structure and conformity. It is also the midpoint of the cycle from one to ten, and represents changes of circumstance, struggle, or obstacles. Change brings new circumstance, so the fives are about adapting or modifying behavior, plans, thoughts, and feelings. Although lack of structure brings uncertainty, flexibility is required because it allows for adjusting behaviors, actions, thoughts, and feelings to achieve what we yearn for and fulfill our destiny.

Five of Wands: This card depicts five young men carrying large wands. It suggests a conflict (business or love). This card also represents little annoyances and road blocks. When these obstacles are overcome, the situation can improve. However, at the moment, nothing appears to be working out.

Upright: Negotiations and competition.

Reversed: Back-stabbing or legal disputes.

Five of Cups: Three cups of wine are spilled, and a person in a dark robe is mourning the loss. However, there are two upright cups behind him, but he does not see them. He can only think about what has been spilled. The card symbolizes remorse. Something has been lost, yet something remains. Because the two upright cups are full, the person must consider what may be saved. Despite the loss, there are two new possible options.

Upright: Disappointment. Something good is about to happen.

Reversed: Unhappiness is a short phase and will end quickly. Be hopeful but cautious.

Five of Swords: Clouds and water together are recurring themes in the Swords suit. Emotions and thoughts are inextricably linked. When anxiety rises, it elicits strong emotions, which can lead to wrong actions. This card represents a victorious person who appears to be invincible, and the other men are forced to surrender their swords to him. The message of this card is to swallow one's pride and accept one's limitations before progressing. The victor stood his ground and won. It also represents that one must stop fighting the wrong battles and try standing one's ground for something that can be won. Currently, he is banging his head against a brick wall, and might be taking on something far too big.

Upright: This card represents an unexpected bad omen (similar to The Tower). However, the situation cannot be avoided. It can imply, for example, the repossession of a home. Underhanded tactics, lies, gossip, or malice could be the cause of your struggle. This card advises you to review your situation and adjust your thoughts or perspective.

Reversed: Strained times are ending soon.

Five of Pentacles: This is the opposite of the customary good luck that comes in the pentacles suit. Here we see two beggars pass beneath an illuminated church window. Five pentacles are shown in the stained-glass window. They are walking in the snow (out in the cold); one of them is lame and feeling ashamed, with a bell hanging around his neck, symbolizing the stigma attached to poverty. The other looks to be homeless and destitute. Because they are hunched in despair, they do not appear to notice the light over their heads. There may be financial anxiety, which is a sign that temporary financial difficulties are on the way.

However, the message might be about more than a shortage of funds. The beggars in this card may have lost their spiritual awareness, as symbolized by their inability to find solace and shelter in the church. The card advises the seeker to pay attention to small things. Money, success, material gain, and happiness are all manifestations of the spiritual understanding needed to create them. Being poor does not equal being spiritual (and spirituality is not about dismissing material wealth). Everything is achieved in balance, and is also transient. When anything of value is not handled with care, it may be lost.

Upright: Serious financial problems. If you have just lost a job, you are capable of regaining control of your finances and finding another one. Your skills, efforts, and hard work will be rewarded.

Reversed: Finances can be restored through hard work and getting back into balance.

6—The Lovers: Collaboration and Service to Others

The Fool receives his first lesson in making his first decision after being nurtured by his parents, The Empress and The Emperor. To do so, he must learn to balance his male and female elements and share the journey with others in a harmonious manner.

The Fool's initial decision-making challenge is represented by The Lovers card. The image depicts a couple standing naked in a garden, beneath an angel. The Fool is facing the woman, who is looking up at the angel. It implies that the male principle of intellect needs the emotional, feminine principle of intuition to connect with Spirit. The relationship's endpoint—the peak—can be seen in the space between them.

The Lovers picture shows that love is more complicated than may appear! If the relationship is to reach new heights, it will require honesty, vulnerability, venturing out of their comfort zone (the garden), and learning to make decisions jointly. The Angel is there to help them maintain harmony. The Lovers show The Fool that joining forces with another person is a conscious decision that will have an impact on his path. The success of the voyage requires a companion with complementary attributes, which is why emotional encounters are crucial for growth. By partnering with others and achieving his goals, The Fool learns to master his ideas and decisions. This card signifies a harmonious union of two people, as well as the courage to be one's genuine self to find true love (or the right partner).

Upright: Love, romance, and emotional, spiritual, and physical union—soulmate. Choices are not crystal clear; use your intuition. If it occurs alongside The Hierophant, it can represent religious marriage, or civil ceremony if the Justice card also appears in the same spread.

Modern Interpretation: Making an important decision that will affect the rest of your life. This card also describes a humanitarian, activist, support-group leader, or someone who specializes in mergers and acquisitions.

Reversed: It is a warning to make the proper choice when choosing a partner. It also represents adultery, sex without love, or relationship difficulties. It indicates a disrupted sex life or jealousy. Moreover, you might be making an irrevocable choice regarding a romantic or work relationship (depending on where it falls in a spread)—so take your time and think carefully.

The Minor Cards—The Sixes

Six represents balance, harmony, and equilibrium. The six-pointed star is made up of two triangles, one pointing up to the sky, or heaven, and the other down to the body, or Earth. This represents a healthy balance as well as the integration of the two aspects. Six also represents romantic and professional relationships. It represents love for another individual as well as love for humankind. Because each decision about a relationship will have long-term consequences, the balance suggests that prudence and awareness are required while making decisions, and the necessity to be guided by Spirit or higher values. Moreover, it represents opposites coming together for the greater good. It also represents the sharing of values that allows two or more people to cooperate and work together.

Six of Wands: A man is depicted on horseback, wearing a laurel wreath, signifying victory and achievement (does this image remind you of the Knight?). His wand has another wreath tied to it. People swarm around him in awe, celebrating his accomplishments. This card represents achievement, the fulfillment of aspirations and wishes, bravery, a successful job, triumph in love, and an overall sense of gratification. Others provide recognition, and success is rewarded with acknowledgment. It denotes a promotion for exemplary work, or a prize for making an effort for a worthy cause.

Upright: Stability and triumph in manifesting or achieving material and creative goals.

Reversed: Indicates losing to the other side (the competition, or other parties). It also indicates trouble at work.

Six of Cups: A little boy presents a flower-filled cup to a young girl, symbolizing friendship (or budding romance). There are five additional cups filled with flowers in front of the two figures. A charming landscape of a village, a thatched cottage, and greenery can be seen around them, evoking warm recollections of home and youth. The Six of Cups indicates a reunion with an old friend or childhood acquaintance, the reappearance of an old sweetheart, or the revival of a love affair with roots in the past. This card might also indicate that something from the past is being reconsidered. The Six of Cups, if misplaced in a spread, might indicate that the seeker is too caught up in the past, or is too sentimental to be practical, and needs to focus on current and future prospective relationships.

Upright: A time of nostalgia and recalling happy times. Reliving childhood memories, connecting with one's inner child or becoming childlike. Meeting old friends from childhood.

Reversed: Loss of innocence or childhood, loss of a childhood friend, letting go of opportunities, cutting binding cords that hold you back.

Six of Swords: The Six of Swords, a suit that frequently shows striving through hardship, represents the delicate balance. A ferryman transports a distraught mother and her infant (the consequence of a broken relationship?) across the sea to a distant land. It's worth noting that the water on the right side of the boat is turbulent, while the water on the left is calm. This denotes a shift away from troubles and into a more serene period. This card can represent a literal voyage, a shift to more attractive surroundings, or the urge to embark on an inner journey. It denotes the release of tension and anxiety following a time of pressure. Harmony and balance will be re-established. Six is associated with assisting others. This card also represents the need to seek assistance, when trapped or suffering, to move forward. Furthermore, it is necessary to stop feeling sorry for oneself. A break, a change of scenery, or stepping back from the issue will provide a fresh perspective.

Upright: Travel across water, away from troubles. A vacation. Time or opportunity to restore harmony and balance.

Reversed: Disappointment, such as a canceled journey. Tenacity and guts are required to resolve your situation.

Six of Pentacles: This card represents six as a harmonious number. A trader is weighing gold to distribute it to the needy. It indicates that money owed will be paid back, or that you will receive what is rightfully yours. Moreover, a kind friend, company, or boss may provide financial assistance. It is a good omen if you are seeking a loan or mortgage. Your financial situation may remain steady for a time. It also suggests sharing your good fortune with others who need financial help or support.

Upright: Generosity from friends or acquaintances. Unexpected financial assistance. Also, it is a message that you've met your financial goals and are encouraged to share your good fortune with others. Giving time and money to good causes brings a great deal of happiness.

Modern interpretation: Successfully securing a loan or a mortgage.

Reversed: Represents a mean or greedy person, stingy behavior, or material loss, such as money or a property.

7—The Chariot: Mind Mastery and Transcendence

The Chariot might be the most mystical card of the Tarot. In its symbols, many secrets are revealed!

Having made the first personal decision about love and relationships, The Fool must now learn to regulate and balance opposing energies within himself to keep a steady course and overcome other issues. Having learned about his dualistic nature through The Lovers card, The Fool realizes that life is a cycle of strife and victory. To overcome outer conflicts, he must first master conflicting forces within himself—namely his mind over his ego.

In contrast to The Lovers card, where he was naked and vulnerable, we see The Fool heavily armored, upright in his vehicle of battle, implying the need to keep the ego in check and connected with an inspired mind, symbolized by the eight-pointed star crown over his head, the blue four-pillar star-spangled canopy. The chariot and the four pillars represent the four elements and the seasonal cycles of change. The star canopy represents the heavens. The Fool appears like the Greek god of war, symbolizing the effort of maintaining the integration of spirit and matter as a human.

Moreover, his chariot is drawn by two sphinxes, one black and one white, which pull the chariot in opposite directions (the result of the union of opposites in the Lovers card). His main task is to keep them under control, symbolizing man's struggle in balancing opposing desires, feelings, and thoughts, as well as the conflict between staying with what is familiar and moving forward. However, no change creates stagnation. Moving forward brings evolution. The Chariot card represents fortitude, which is required to move forward in balance. Conflicts are necessary to bring about change and growth.

Furthermore, look closely and you will notice that there are no reins attached to the sphinxes. They are masterminded by The Fool, who seems to be cemented in his chariot (from the bottom down). And, although the chariot is made of heavy stones, it has somehow crossed over water onto land. Additionally, The Fool's (or charioteer's) garment is embellished with mystical symbols: secret writings and an enigmatic sash denoting full control over his instinctual desires. The focus is on the intellect and the mind, symbolized by the white shining square across his chest; the two crescents on his shoulders, pointing to heaven, symbolize his receptive intuition to spiritual guidance. This is further enforced by the red bolt on the chariot's shield, with a winged disk on top.

He is in control and balanced, as he holds the wand of The Magician in his right arm. All refer to the mystical knowledge he received from each of the characters we've met. Intuition and logic, creativity and methodology, feminine and masculine, spiritual and material aspects are integrated and in balance. This card signifies The Fool's triumphant crowning for his achievements. He has transcended the duality and constraints of the nature of man.

Upright: At this point in life, you must be practical and apply your developed skills and mental focus to overcome problems. This card represents triumph. Hard work is about to be rewarded. Overnight success, material gain. News or friends from afar. Your inner gifts are about to emerge. Don't fuss—get on with it!

Modern Interpretation: Strategist, high-level problem solver, visionary, innovator, specializes in overseas expansion.

Reversed: Lack of discipline, situation out of control. Addiction, envy, avarice. Afraid to use abilities. Arrogance or lack of self-confidence. Burying head in the sand. Warning against overwhelming ambition, burnout, or wasting resources.

Minor Cards: The Sevens
Seven represents completion, completeness, safety, victory, and rest after achieving

a milestone. It is a mystical number that represents wisdom and spiritual growth. There are seven notes on a musical scale, seven colors in the rainbow, and seven planets in traditional astrology. We are in a state of happiness and balance when we are in "seventh heaven." It's like the feeling of relief after a long exhale.

Seven of Wands: Purpose and value are two attributes of 7—both of which are depicted on this card. The Seven of Wands depicts a brave man with a wand fighting six other wands that rise to attack him. It symbolizes competition and conflict that appears overwhelming at first. However, the man stays focused on his purpose, and triumphs. The card indicates that a career change is likely; however, strength and determination are required to achieve success. It is also possible that competition will be confronted in business, but perseverance and courage will triumph in the end. This card represents knowledge and incorporates skills. It can represent an excellent teacher, training, lecturing, or writing.

Upright: When success is followed by stiff competition, show perseverance and courage to overcome difficulties. Success is assured (if you persevere).

Reversed: Time to retreat and wait for an opportune moment; opportunities thrown away due to fear.

Seven of Cups: The Seven of Cups represents a man with a vivid imagination. Seven cups appear from the clouds floating before him. He stands perplexed, unsure which one to select: the castle, the jewels, the victory wreath, the dragon, the curly-haired woman, or the snake. However, draped in the center is a figure with a halo in a cup. This represents his true self, which has yet to be revealed. The card suggests that a decision must be made with care. Otherwise, his dreams and ideas will remain castles in the clouds. Unless one of the cups is chosen, nothing will be achieved. It's a time when the imagination runs wild and soul options seem numerous. Confusion over the decision is accompanied by an abundance of creative and artistic talent, and energy that can be directed in a positive way.

Upright: There is a lot of creativity and talent around this situation, but there is also a lot of confusion. Decisions about creative and relationship matters must be made, no matter how difficult they are. You are confused because there is so much choice. This is not the time for daydreaming; your imagination is too vivid. Need to be realistic.

Reversed: Loss of opportunity; dangerous delusions.

Seven of Swords: A man appears to be fleeing from a camp in the background with a bundle of five swords. Two swords remain embedded in the ground behind him. As he sneaks away, there is a guilty expression on his face, and he looks over his shoulder. This card represents the need for caution and staying away from temptation to achieve your goal. Direct or aggressive tactics will be ineffective. Diplomacy and charm will be potent. If the card is badly placed, a flight from a dishonorable act is advised.

Upright: Think carefully, tactfully, and diplomatically. Aiming for goals aggressively will not work, nor would being overly hostile. Caution must be taken because deception is likely.

Reversed: Get professional advice; otherwise, you may lose out. Be cautious of burglary and superficial contacts.

Seven of Pentacles: A young farmer is depicted leaning on his hoe. He seems to have the skills to gather his harvest, and he has done good, solid work. The seven days of labor are over, yet he pauses from work, assessing his harvest and dreaming about what needs to be done, wondering if it is good enough. This card indicates a pause in a business or an enterprise and warns against stopping for too long. Previous efforts will only be successful if they are consistent.

Upright: Financial choices and decisions. Fortitude is required. Yo u are about to enter a challenging period, but don't lose hope; instead, pick yourself up and make the required changes after a break. The pause will help you find a new avenue to pursue.

Reversed: Giving up easily, or constantly worrying about money or career without acting. Has skills but won't work. Discipline, focus and consistent work is advised.

PHASE 2: INNER ALCHEMY (CARDS 8–14)

The Fool has now grasped the concept of complementary opposites. He's also learned that he can achieve his goals by honing his skills, collaborating with others, and mastering his ego and mind.

Instead of overcoming conflicts, The Chariot teaches him to apply mental mastery of his ego and connect with his higher purpose.

The Fool's next stage of growth entails confronting the complexities of being human. It entails delving deep into his inner world to find balance, control, maturity and a higher purpose. In addition, he begins to understand the impermanent nature of life, short cycles of unexpected change, and unavoidable transitions. Choices have consequences, and he must learn that stepping away to reflect is necessary before continuing his journey. If he doesn't, life will force him to.

8—Justice: Balance and Legal Matters

Despite the universe's apparent randomness, its structure contains a certain justice or fairness that reflects the need for balance and harmony in our lives. The Justice card underlines The Fool's karmic lesson: actions have consequences for which he must take responsibility. With Justice, inner transformation begins as the ego, or the personality, aligns with the intentions and higher motives of the consciousness when one makes decisions that impact others.

The Justice card implies that opposing viewpoints are always present. The scales represent the feminine principle of passive evaluation, while the sword represents the masculine principle of decision and action. Justice's message is that when opposing forces work together, the right decision can be made. Choices also have consequences, as they cause change. Justice teaches The Fool that making the right choice entails making a decision based on facts after weighing all the factors. Justice was reassigned to number 8 by Waite in the second edition of the Rider-Waite-Smith pack. Can you see how this is relevant to Justice?

Justice indicates that, even though circumstances may be dictated, mastering and balancing emotions is critical to making the fairest decision. The Justice figure is an androgynous-looking, unbiased figure who exhibits a dispassionate but discriminate and fair intellect. The purple veil behind Justice represents the wisdom of making fair decisions. To achieve harmony, balancing opposites necessitates a well-balanced mind. The choice must be made by balancing heart and mind, as symbolized by Justice's red and green robes and the solid stone throne on which he sits.

The red circle inside the white square around his neck denotes passion and spirit, respectively—the result is balance and harmony. If you look closely at the card, you'll notice that Justice's right hand is pointing upward, toward Spirit, while his left hand, which is holding the scale, is pointing toward Earth, symbolizing spiritual wisdom applied practically to material life on Earth (a mature, older Magician). The one foot of Justice sticking out from beneath the robes, pointing to material life, embodies higher wisdom applied to everyday living.

Upright: When opposing forces are in harmony, the appropriate decision can be made; choices have consequences since they cause change. You are advised to consider that making the right decision requires evaluation of your situation using intellect and facts—not emotions. The situation requires you to be honest and fair. Have courage and connect with your conviction before making decisions. Being resolute and grounded is required, integrating conscious and subconscious. It also denotes a generous and fair-minded person, or a favorable settlement of legal matters, contracts, or negotiations. It can indicate choice or decision—logic. Balanced, fair, clear-sighted view of life. Indicates accountants, judges, lawyers, and people who make laws.

Modern Interpretation: Legal (if The Hierophant appears in the same spread, and The Lovers) and civil marriages (The Lovers). Signing of contracts, a legal battle that ends fairly, signing of legal documents to establish a contract or a business.

Reversed: If making unreasonable demands, you may get less than you hope. It indicates complications in legal matters, injustice, imbalance, and delays. Major adjustments are needed to balance life. A divorce or separation, dissolution of partnerships.

Minor Cards—The Eights

Eight represents regeneration and the balancing of opposing forces. It symbolizes the death of the old, which is evil or wrong, and the birth of the new, which is pure and just. It allows situations to be modified, as well as addressing what was out of balance, unfair, or unjust. Eight acts as a thruster. Decisions will have a cascading effect that will be felt almost immediately. To grow in wisdom, one must die a little each day, letting go of old ideas, habits, and ways of thinking.

Eight of Wands: This card depicts eight wands flying across the sky, passing over the peaceful countryside. It represents

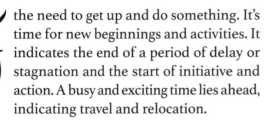

the need to get up and do something. It's time for new beginnings and activities. It indicates the end of a period of delay or stagnation and the start of initiative and action. A busy and exciting time lies ahead, indicating travel and relocation.

Upright: Sudden movement, or air travel. A new location. New developments in a situation that was stagnant.

Reversed: Delay in travel plans. Caution against making hasty decisions, resulting in mistakes.

Eight of Cups: A man walks away from eight cups, demonstrating his concern over a relationship he thought about considerably (because they're neatly stacked). However, he abandons them and heads toward a mountain, symbolizing his determination to find a new destination or relationship (no matter how far it is). The moon is in both full and waning quarters, indicating the end of one cycle and the start of another. The card represents letting go of the past, abandoning a situation due to disappointment or disillusionment. Although thought and effort have gone into a situation or a relationship, it is not right, and the seeker has no choice but to leave.

Upright: Change of heart, moving in a new direction emotionally. Let go of old habits and emotions and embrace new ones.

Reversed: A person following a fantasy, not seeing the reality of their situation but indulging in emotions. Situation can lead to depression. Stagnating due to indulging emotions without rational thinking and considering facts.

Eight of Swords: A woman appears to be stranded on a marsh, surrounded by eight swords planted in the water. Behind her, a large castle can be seen in the distance, symbolizing a better place, where she would be safe, dry, and protected. The card appears bleak, but it is her fears, her refusal to confront the situation, and her inability to make decisions that keep her imprisoned. The card's message is to be brave when faced with problems and to face them head on. You can't be paralyzed by your fears forever.

Upright: Stalemate situation, or trapped conditions. The constraints that this card implies are frequently self-imposed, and persist due to fear and indecision. Positive action has the power to end the stagnation.

Reversed: Gradually seeing the light. Getting answers, or releasing fear, anxiety, and indecision.

Eight of Pentacles: Pentacles are being carved by an apprentice craftsman. He appears to be enthusiastic about his work, the results of which are nailed to the block of wood in front of him. When the energy of 8 is combined with this card, it symbolizes talent and skills. It can indicate the possibility of turning such a skill into a profession, or the possibility of earning money through it. Although things are still in the apprentice stage, do not let that hold you back. There is the possibility of new employment in the skilled field. Hard work and practical ideas are the solid foundations for establishing a new and lucrative career, both emotionally and financially.

Upright: Skills will bring financial rewards. Patience. A new project has begun. This card represents learning and mastering new skills, which can lead to a new means of earning income or pursuing a new project. On the other hand, financial prosperity is predicted, and now is the time to maintain your composure and faith in your talents.

Reversed: Indicates disorganization and problems in a project, a business, or finances. Overwhelmed by having too much to do.

9—The Hermit: Withdrawal and Reflection

The Hermit is the wise spiritual mentor or teacher, a lone traveler who lights the way for other travelers. He promotes The Fool's growth by digging into spiritual understanding beyond personal gain. Larger decisions necessitate a period of seclusion, meditation, and withdrawal. Before continuing his quest, The Fool must confront his insecurities. The Hermit requires patience, as opposed to Justice, who must act quickly and equitably. This signifies that wisdom is achieved via the use of a clear, thoughtful mind. After some time alone, The Fool realizes that there is more to life than what happens in the hectic, distracted outer world.

The Hermit symbolizes The Fool grown up. The Hermit is typically depicted as an elderly man with a long, white beard, cloaked and hooded, and carrying a lamp. It represents the archetype of the wise elderly man; in the Tarot he is, in fact, The Fool who is getting older. The Hermit bridges youth and old age. In his youth, The Fool leaps off the brink of a cliff in broad daylight, his face elevated and his staff lightly held. The older and wiser Hermit has learned many valuable lessons, and now walks with caution and relies on his staff (Wand) for support. He is frequently shown carrying a lantern, figuratively illuminating the darkness for others as his eyes are closed (in confidence). As he continues his solitary journey over snow, his heavy cloak and hood protect him from the cold.

Hermits typically reside in monasteries or hermitages; however, in the Tarot, The Hermit is frequently seen in a landscape, implying that he is still looking for a spot to rest. This also represents the never-ending pursuit of wisdom. The journey here is an inner one of reflection rather than a physical one—in other words, withdrawing from society to gain enlightenment. Furthermore, alchemical thought is frequently used in the quest for personal transformation and enlightenment. The first half of our life journey is usually about achieving security and worldly gain, while the second half is a search for self-knowledge and self-reflection that begins with The Hermit. Today's fast-paced lifestyle makes it difficult to devote time to introspection. We are increasingly pressed to find immediate solutions. While our outward world is continuously changing, our internal reality is not.

Upright: Traveling allows you to gain experience. There is always something new and fresh to discover about life. This card also asks you to withdraw into isolation to reflect on and learn from your experiences. The wisdom of life's obstacles will be revealed if you take time to understand. You'll have a better grasp of your life and be able to share your wisdom with others, enlightening them. Worldly affairs can be distracting, so use caution and take your time when deciding on issues that matter—discreetly. It also indicates that you may feel you have accomplished everything you set out to do, and are wondering what's next. However, more knowledge or experience is required.

Reversed: Enforced loneliness. Immaturity and superficiality, life full of empty chatter. Do not reject advice given to you. Pig-headedness, refusal to listen. Wasting time. Examine your life and preoccupations. Reconnect with friends.

Modern Interpretation: Professor, researcher, philosopher, mentor, specialized publisher, historian, experienced therapist, wise intellectual.

Minor Cards—The Nines
Before starting a new cycle with the Ace,

you must complete nine rounds. It denotes the end of one phase and the start of a new one (Ace). The number 9 represents resurrection, and things that need to be gathered before completion. It also represents the culmination of all previous stages, such as preparation, knowledge-gathering, and skill-honing. It represents laying a solid foundation before the tenth step, which is the final completion.

Nine of Wands: This is a card of determination and strength. As if defending his territory, a man stands ready. He has already fought, as seen by his bandaged head, but he's still willing and ready to fight for what he values. It implies that even when you think you've exhausted your abilities, there's strength in reserve. It places the seeker in a powerful position and suggests victory through perseverance and carriage.

Upright: Need to be flexible, not obstinate or rigid in thinking.

Reversed: Loss of position, drive, or strength. Afraid to lose status.

Nine of Cups: This is the wish card; it represents the fulfillment of a major desire. Nine upright cups form an arch behind a well-dressed man who sits with his arms crossed. He appears to be happy and well-fed, feeling physically and emotionally safe. It denotes emotional stability as well as physical and material happiness. Sensual pleasures are met too.

Upright: Wishes would come true. Beneficial.

Reversed: Beware of feeling smug. Delay in fulfillment of wishes.

Nine of Swords: This card looks worse than what it represents. A sleepless woman sits up in bed holding her head in her hands, anticipating doom. She seems to be in despair. Next to her, nine swords are suspended, and on her bed panel two swordsmen are fighting. The signs of the zodiac embroidered on her quilt indicate that she has been feeling this way for a long time. However, the swords do not touch her, indicating that her fears are unfounded, and may be caused by negative thinking. Covering her eyes, she indicates that she is not facing her situation. Her fears are worse than the reality of the situation. Extreme stress is indicated, and it's making her lose sleep. Nonetheless, no matter how difficult it seems, she must face her fears and decide as swiftly as the swords, because her worries are paralyzing, and far worse than the outcome.

Upright: Distress, mental stress or illness, nightmares, fear, and anxiety due to overthinking and worrying, which might lead to feeling oppressed.

Reversed: Lessening of situation. Light at the end of the tunnel.

Nine of Pentacles: This card represents someone who can enjoy wonderful things while in solitude. In a blooming vineyard, a well-dressed woman stands alone in the garden of her manifested reality. The falcon on her gloved hand denotes that her thoughts are under control. A manor house in the background represents material wealth and the vastness of the land she owns. The card represents delighting in physical comfort and financial achievement. It does not suggest that the person is literally without relationships.

Not only does the person love her own company, she is also at peace with herself, grateful to enjoy what she has; she doesn't necessarily require companionship to feel complete. Moreover, there's a snail in the foreground that symbolizes slow, methodical, consistent effort, which yields results. There is no attachment to material

gain, rather enjoying the fruits of her labor. Financial and material advantages are anticipated and cherished.

Upright: Material prosperity. Windfall. Comfortable retirement. You are about to start a new phase of your life, one in which you have attained financial independence and security. You no longer need to work. This card portends that your hard work and dedication will be rewarded shortly.

Reversed: Self-absorbed, and consequently suffering financial risks.

10—Wheel of Fortune: Unexpected Change of Fortune

The Fool learns from The Wheel of Fortune that much of life appears to be random, with unanticipated, quick changes and opportunities. There are many ups and downs in life. He recognizes that the one constant in life is change.

All situations will ebb and flow continuously. He learns to respect the seasons and the cycle of life, and therefore the right timing for action. Moreover, he learns to persevere in hard times, for these, too, will come to an end. In other words, there are forces beyond his control.

The Wheel of Fortune represents both stability and change. As a result, The Fool must be willing to accept and adapt to change, which builds his personal and emotional resilience. This is a significant step in his inner transformation. The period of seclusion and introspection rapidly gives way to a period of progress and development. Consequently, caution is required to be attentive and in the present moment, ready to adapt and act in response to developments. Like The Moon, the wheel is round and ever-changing.

Although this card appears as a light-hearted bringer of good fortune, it is perhaps the card that contains the most alchemical symbols, emphasizing the cycles of self-transformation on various levels. Waite asked for the Wheel of Fortune card to be illustrated with a blend of Egyptian and biblical figures, emphasizing the notion of death and rebirth. The snake on the left represents Seth, the Egyptian god who introduced death to the Earth and assassinated the noble king Osiris. Anubis, the jackal-headed figure on the right, is a guide to deceased souls and a bringer of new life. On top, a sphinx representing Horus, son of Osiris and god of Resurrection, is depicted. The zodiac is another wheel depicting the cycle of death and rebirth—gain via loss and vice versa. The four animals in each corner appear to be inspired by Ezekiel's biblical vision (*Ezekiel* 1:10). They also reflect the astrological fixed elements of Taurus, Leo, Scorpio, and Aquarius, which symbolize earth, fire, water, and air, respectively.

Another depiction of a vast, ever-revolving wheel that indicates a passage through time by season is the zodiac. The elements represent those used in alchemy, and the symbols on the wheel's spokes are similarly alchemical. From top to bottom, clockwise, they read: mercury, sulfur, water, and salt. The combination of the four elements results in a perfect fifth—continuity and flow.

The card's message is that through constant renewal, and cycles of death and rebirth, the inner self evolves and transforms to create a perfect state of harmony between heaven and Earth. The Wheel of Fortune also depicts the inner driving force that is formed when the cycles of time turn. The Wheel of Fortune informs us that, while changes are vital for growth and moving life forward, it is up to us, the individual, to adapt, change, and evolve.

The hub of the wheel remains stationary as the rim rotates, depicting time marching on, year after year, season after season. The Sun, Moon, and planets are always revolving, circling around the zodiac wheel, yet the wheel is always the same. Life is made up of cycles of change that symbolize opposing aspects such as day and night, expansion and contraction. In the second stage of metamorphosis, The Fool has begun to experience those profound cycles. This card's message is also indicating the necessity of change to bring about transformation.

If you will, it is our deep, or unconscious, personality that frequently invites a change of situation. Although we may not always it, we can typically perceive the opportunity for growth that it entails, or blame life! As a result, the more you learn about yourself, the more freedom you will have. In a reading, The Wheel of Fortune represents a shift in circumstances. We may or may not want it, but it is critical that we respond to change. Whatever we do, the wheel turns The Chariot's triumph into misfortune, and then back into victory in a never-ending cycle.

Upright: Fortunate coincidences, quick changes, external influences, fortunate meetings, and lucky breaks shape your life. The wheel has turned, and you are beginning a new cycle; unexpected opportunities are likely. Although it is a positive card, matters are in a state of flux, and you may feel confused. It is important not to resist this phase, and when the dust settles, you may find new friends, career, a new home, or income. The Wheel of Fortune represents influences that can change the outcome of a circumstance. Regardless of the constraints, this card represents a breakthrough or unexpected change, such as meeting someone new, or getting a job offer, depending on where it falls in a spread.

Reversed: Bad luck dogs your path. Be patient; the wheel is always in motion and fate will smile once again. It's a bad time to initiate new projects or gamble on things going in your favor. Unexpected delays. Change is usually positive at the end. Expect the unexpected.

Minor Cards—The Tens

Ten is associated with completeness and perfection. A 10-step procedure was required for the 9 cycle to finish. In the number 10, one represents the beginning, and zero represents the spirit, before returning to a new cycle of one again. Ten allows the current cycle of preparation to finish. In the Minor Arcana of Cups and Pentacles, 10 represents the pinnacle of bliss and happiness, whereas the Swords and Wands represent trial and tribulation.

Ten of Wands: A young man walks awkwardly and uncomfortably toward his home in the distance, grasping ten blossoming wands. He appears to be physically exhausted, but he continues to walk steadily toward his objective. This card indicates that a load is about to be lifted or an issue is about to be solved. Oppression, on the other hand, is frequently self-imposed, and the seeker can do a lot to lighten his load. The weight can be physical, mental, or emotional, but something can be done to ease the strain. This card indicates excessive initiatives taken to the point of self-burdening. The point of the lesson The Fool is learning from this card is that, regardless of the difficulties he carries alone, there are times when it is beneficial to listen to others' advice. Take time to examine your life, when your personal burden becomes unbearable, to ensure that you are still on the right track.

Upright: Avoid neglecting physical limitations; if you don't set clear boundaries, you risk being overburdened. Too much pressure can lead to sickness. Movement with responsibility. This card also represents the burdens of ambition.

Reversed: End of a period of hard work. Welcome new responsibilities that will lead to a promotion.

Ten of Cups: A young married couple stands arm in arm, holding hands and raising their arms to heaven in joy. Ten gleaming cups form an arch above them, resembling a rainbow. Two children are joyously dancing together nearby. Over the hills, we can see the family home, which is surrounded by trees. The number 10 represents perfection, and this card represents a beautiful family life and long-term contentment. As the cups are made in the heavens above, their happiness stems from emotional security as well as spiritual connection. This card indicates that you are at a high point in your personal relationships and that you are experiencing harmony in all areas of your life. Your wishes and ambitions have been realized. It might also signify the start of a new cycle. Recognize the work you and others have done to achieve your goals, but remain open to new possibilities so your happiness can be long-lasting and continuous.

Upright: After a long period of hard work, this is a time of contentment and fulfillment. Good luck due to perseverance. A special happy event (marriage, childbirth, child's birthday), or lasting happiness.

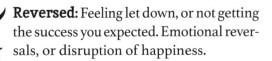

Reversed: Feeling let down, or not getting the success you expected. Emotional reversals, or disruption of happiness.

Ten of Swords: A man lies dead on the ground, his back gravely wounded by ten swords plunged into it. The tragedy is heightened by the dark and ominous sky above. The dying man's right-hand fingers are bent and touching each other in a ritual gesture that suggests completion. Even though this card initially appears to represent a violent death, it is actually about profound loss. If this card appears in a spread, you may be feeling a loss in your personal life or work; however, there is another interpretation.

Perhaps a part of you has died suddenly, but you're now receptive to something fresh and energizing. The number 10 represents completion, but also growth on a higher level—just as death also represents rebirth. Your lower ego self must die for your higher self to experience spiritual awakening. This marks the end of one chapter and the start of a new one. Before you can progress, you must let go of old, outdated patterns of thinking.

Upright: Disappointment, disillusion, and false hope clear the decks for a fresh outlook, truth, and clarity. Deception,

treachery, or stress may lead to physical illness when understanding is lacking.

Reversed: Recovery from illness. Negative thinking must change. Change your attitude—it is holding you back.

Ten of Pentacles: A well-dressed, elderly man—the family patriarch—sits, with two loyal dogs at his knee. An adjacent archway bears his coat of arms, and two more members of the family, a young man and a woman, greet each other joyfully nearby. The image appears to be one of clan or family unity, based on many years of tradition. The spheres of the Kabbalistic Tree of Life are superimposed on this medieval family setting, reminding us that we are members of both a family and a community, and that while we seek physical well-being and prosperity, spiritual fulfillment is also important. This card represents long-term success based on spiritual wisdom. The card's message is that acquiring material gain through a balanced attitude lasts for generations.

Upright: The formation of sturdy foundations for families or businesses is indicated. The purchase of a home, for example, or the establishment of a tradition, are symbolic of security, stability, and permanence. Family money (legacy). Renewal. Financial comfort. You will get used to living in luxury, but be careful not to grow complacent and overindulgent. Long-term prosperity and material contentment have been achieved. You are at ease in your house and will be in a position to leave a wonderful legacy to your descendants.

Modern interpretation: A store, boutique, restaurant, department mall, business headquarters, office, or luxurious home.

Reversed: Laziness, or a person who is lazy. Too much luxury stopping you from making real achievements. Family money or financial misfortune.

11—Strength: The Healer

This card represents the female aspect of The Hermit, the wise feminine "sagess." She advises The Fool to trust his inner power, increase his confidence, and use his limitless inner resources to oppose human cravings. He learns to control his higher mind over his lower appetites, as well as tame his wants while remaining spiritually connected to his bigger purpose. The Fool learns to lovingly control his cravings as he meets his feminine spiritual mentor. She is symbolized by Strength gently taming the masculine lion, which also represents masculine drive. The lesson is that true strength and power come from being gentle, and in command of our cravings and sexual desires.

There is no use of undue force or aggression about this strength. It's all about feminine charm and tenderness. Strength teaches The Fool spiritual alchemy or self-transformation on a higher level, as The Empress did with gentle and caring love. Now that The Fool's inner and exterior resources are in balance, he is poised to achieve greater heights. This is achieved by surrendering his "old self," as he learned from The Wheel of Fortune and will learn from The Hanged Man. He must give up old methods of perceiving, thinking, and acting for The Wheel of Fortune to turn in his favor.

The image of a human battling the King of Beasts appears in several Tarot decks, and represents man's fight to control his animal impulses. Strength can refer to both inner and physical strength. It echoes the conflict between man and lion, portraying the feminine aspect of dealing with the opposing lions portrayed by The Chariot—the struggle between instinctual desires and the conscious mind. In The Chariot card, the masculine aspect is represented by The Fool wearing a talisman "skirt" around his genitals to control his ego and physical urges, which could impede or distract him from winning his battle. He is on high alert, summoning all his physical might and abilities to win. In the Strength card, by contrast, a woman is wearing a floral garland around her waist that cascades down to the ground, spiraling across her abdomen as she gently seals the lion's mouth. This is higher-level personal alchemy, or self-transformation.

Both cards suggest that our higher spiritual nature can triumph over earthly wants by conquering the lion. The woman wears flowers in her hair and is taming the lion and placing a garland around its neck in the Strength card. The woman, like The Empress, has golden hair and wears a white gown to symbolize spiritual purity. She is taming the lion with ease, demonstrating the power of spiritual intuition over force. In the second phase, it means that The Fool has undergone a more profound metamorphosis, symbolizing control over any remnants of the animal soul that may still exist in a person's consciousness. The maiden, who represents the moon and femininity, is depicted beside the lion, who represents the sun and masculinity. We got a glimpse of The Fool's youth as we went through the Major cards. He had his first training from The Magician; we met his earthly parents, The Empress and The Emperor, and then his spiritual guides or heavenly parents, The High Priestess and The Hierophant. We learned about The Fool's struggles and vulnerability when he fell in love in The Lovers card, and he mastered his thoughts and feelings to find balance and continue conquering opposites in The Chariot card. When he gets to Justice, he has to do more than just act and respond. He needed to think objectively. The Hermit urged him to look for meaning. With The Wheel of Fortune, his mindset shifts even more as he realizes that he remains vulnerable. He could rise and fall, but it is out of his control because such are the cycles of life. Now he needs Strength to provide him with the self-control, dignity, and courage to confront the next phase of the journey to the underworld.

Drawing this card indicates that you have triumphed over fears or anxieties. It's time to master your resources and energies in preparation for the next chapter of your journey. Moreover, future success will be realized more easily through evolved understanding, love, and compassion (toward other people and sentient beings, including animals) in your everyday life.

Upright: Better times are on the way! This is your chance to prove your inner strength and wisdom. You will prevail over life's hardships if you have the fortitude to endure. A beloved animal could enter your life. If you have relationship difficulties, open your heart, forgive, and forget. Besotted with an older woman. Recovering from illness.

Modern Interpretation: Healing on a deep level. A person who has healing abilities. Animal communication skills. Someone who specializes in conflict resolution. Accomplished personality. Woman of substance and impact, who is charismatic, self-assured, and grounded. A mentor.

Reversed: Fear and weakness are barriers to success. Your inner strength will help you overcome difficult situations. Someone who is not in control of their instincts and sexual desires.

12—The Hanged Man: Surrender and Sacrifice

The Fool learns from The Hanged Man that certain answers can be found if one stops looking for them, surrenders, and accepts his predicament. The Fool can see things from a fresh perspective by hanging upside down! To be set free from suspension, The Fool must give up his previous way of life to be enlightened. The Fool recognizes the need to let go, to separate from the materialistic rut he created for himself, to fully understand the spiritual wisdom that lies beneath his "suspended" state.

The Hanged Man represents another form of death, change, or transformation; this time it is forced upon The Fool to help him prepare for the next phase. He must mature by giving up the childish ways and attitudes of earlier life. Effectively, he is learning to give up his ego, and be guided to a more meaningful existence. The "incarceration" is forced upon him to teach him the lesson of sacrifice. He must reach a state of deeper self-awareness, depicted by the halo around his head, and recognize that the past must change. A new cycle of growth demands a renewed attitude and maturity.

Traitors were sometimes killed upside down by the Italians in medieval times. In Renaissance Italy, people used a type of graffiti known as "shame paintings." If they didn't like a local ruler, they would create an upside-down cartoon of him on a wall, often hanging by one foot. The card is known as The Traitor in several Italian decks, and depicts a person contorted with pain, arms outstretched and bent, as if flailing. Coins occasionally fall from his pocket.

However, if we consider the nameless and unnumbered card from the Visconti-Sforza Tarot of 1450—probably the earliest version of Major Arcana cards we know of—The Hanged Man is depicted as an elegant young man with his hands behind his back and a calm expression on his face. The card depicts tranquility rather than pain. Traditionally, the image of The Hanged Man in the Tarot is represented by an unusual figure hanging upside down by one foot. Despite his awkward position, his face is calm and composed, giving the image a soothing effect.

The card implies that The Fool must take this upside-down position to gain perspective (not punishment), and attain a new degree of insight. The Fool has fought the lion, his shadow-self, with the Strength card. He realized he could identify with more than his conscious self. He is aware that he has an unconscious side that he is only beginning to understand. The Hanged Man signifies the start of his journey into the unconscious (the third phase) as well as his preparation for the next and last stage of his development and fulfillment.

Moreover, The Hanged Man portrays a man suspended from a tree trunk, with leaves spreading across the two ends, implying a dynamic image of growing life—a continuous evolution. The Hanged Man is hanging in the middle of the trunk, signifying the balance he must strike between the conscious and unconscious mind. His crossed leg forms an inverted triangle, pointing downward, toward the unconscious. The Fool sees the world from a different perspective when he's upside down. The card represents yet another opportunity to bring opposites together to achieve enlightenment.

When The Hanged Man appears in a reading, it's a period of personal choice. Something of personal value must be given up, achieving something of even greater value. Because there is no assurance of outcome for what The Fool might leap into next, this sacrifice requires faith. As a result, the sacrifice must be made without the expectation of a reward—only the hope that it will be worthy.

Upright: The inability to move forward due to a temporary pause or suspension. However, other people's input and behaviors are also a part of the delay (others tied The Hanged Man to the tree trunk). This is not the best time to decide; there will be delays. So patience is required as well as a reevaluation of your intentions. Moreover, you will need to "sacrifice" your old ways, to reinvent yourself. Something must be lost before you can make your way forward; otherwise, this status quo will continue.

Modern Interpretation: Opportunity to reset your life. You will emerge from this period with renewed energy.

Reversed: Warning against selfishness and materialism. The person in the reading might have neglected their spiritual growth and their unconscious programming or actions, and is preoccupied with material life. Holding on to the past and failing to grasp new opportunities. Bad investments, loss of belongings, and reversals of fortune. Stop and think. Do not let others pressure you into getting involved.

13—Death: Inevitable End and a New Beginning

Death is the final letting go, the ultimate shift in The Fool's makeover. It represents transition, renewal, the end of old ways, and the death of the past, the end of relationships, even home or environment, that

The Fool has accomplished—all of which indicate a change that must happen. The Fool discovers how mysterious, secretive, healing, and regenerating the end of old ways can be.

Death is shown in the Tarot through a dramatic image. Death as a skeleton rides a white horse and is clad in black. Black is the color of death because it absorbs all color, just as Death absorbs all life. White represents spiritual purity since it obliterates or blends all colors.

The next thing we notice is that a skeleton is riding the horse. This is a metaphor for the body's hardest and most resistant part; flesh does not endure, but bone remains. It symbolizes the stripping away of material possessions. Death is symbolized by a white horse riding roughshod over a king (in the Rider-Waite-Smith deck) and stepping over his toppled crown. This imagery expresses that no earthly kingdom lasts. The horse rejects the Bishop's pleas for mercy, while the maiden is forced to turn her head away from the inevitable. It demonstrates that death is indiscriminate.

The sun rises in the background, a sign of hope and resurrection, between the two pillars symbolizing life's duality. The sun also symbolizes the start of a new cycle or a new dawn. This is another reference to the human evolutionary cycle, implying that death is unavoidable. When the natural cycle of change is resisted, suffering is the result. Behind Death we see a boat on a river, whose waters flow toward a new life, symbolized by green scenery and reeds growing on the riverbank. This symbolizes that death is necessary to create and regenerate life. On the forebank of the river we see death and a ruined, arid land. On the other bank we see how the river of death also feeds and generates a new life.

In a reading, Death can signify the end of things in a variety of ways. Death, for example, may show in the spread of someone who is about to be married, as it represents the end of life as a single person, or in the spread of someone about to be divorced, representing the end of married life. The presence of the Death card could also represent leaving school, leaving a job or leaving a country, none of which indicate physical death. The Death card in the Tarot is associated with transition and change rather than literal death.

Willingness or reluctance to surrender to an impending transformation correlates to the degree of suffering experienced under the influence of the Death card. Death can indicate sadness or a welcome relief, depending on the seeker's circumstances. Nonetheless, it needs to be acknowledged as the ending, mourned or honored, just as the ancient Greeks honored Death by paying the ferryman.

Allow yourself time to examine, digest, and integrate the changes brought on by the Death card. There is no right time assigned to the grieving process, as long as the river of life keeps moving you forward. For Death, in its essential meaning, is about decay.

Upright: Major changes lie ahead, and you may need time to mourn the passing of what you are leaving behind. Loss of some kind: a relationship fails; a friendship ends; a job is lost. Transformation ahead; renewal and the start of a new life. This card teaches The Fool that the old ways are doomed and that he must change. He is transformed as he comes to terms with loss. According to its position in a spread, Death might represent a change of relationship or home.

Modern Interpretation: Imperative changes that are outside of your control (usually endings) affect new beginnings.

Reversed: Resisting change; life very boring. Lethargy and inertia. Stagnation.

Unable to adjust to new circumstances.

14—Temperance: Harmony, Negotiations and Agreements

This card represents the transformed Fool, having confronted Death. He emerges with a sense of balance, elegance, integrity, and moderation. As though some divine alchemical process has taken place, he now finds peace and harmony bridging the conflict of accepting the renewal process of life. The Fool has learned to manage his thoughts (The Emperor, The Chariot) and feelings (Strength), and can relate harmoniously to others. The message of this card is that the key to resolving any conflict is through forgiveness and compromise.

The image of the Temperance card is usually of an angelic figure pouring liquid from one cup into another. Temperance refers to a state of moderation. The Temperance angel stands near a pool, one foot in the water and the other on the rocks, symbolizing continuity between past and future, conscious and unconscious, the subconscious and higher consciousness, as well as the spiritual and earthly worlds (remember the foot sticking out in the Justice card?). The angel represents the present, and heavenly intervention, which serves as a bridge between the spiritual and physical worlds. The angel's head is illuminated by a golden halo, and the circle with the red dot in the center represents eternity and the continuation of the life-cycle; Spirit is the starting point that drives all material life.

A triangle within a square may be found on its chest, symbolizing the significance of reaching out to a higher mind, or Spirit, for inspirational guidance that drives a secure material life. The symbolism of the golden crown rising above the snow-covered mountains, which represent material or worldly triumphs, reinforces this concept by expressing that enduring achievements begin with seeking spiritual guidance or manifesting in partnership with Spirit. It encourages balance between spirituality and earthly achievements, the conscious and unconscious self, higher mind and subconscious mind, and the emotions. When the river of emotions flows freely, it nurtures the life flourishing on its banks, rather than flooding, which results in chaos.

Transferring the liquid of emotions between the two cups is a metaphor expressing the alchemical process that takes place as two people or two parties exchange their feelings honestly. When words are spoken from the heart, they are received by the heart. So feelings are fluid, and need to flow or be expressed openly and in balance to achieve harmonious relationships. In the same way that Justice (an air card) necessitates a balanced intellect, Temperance (a water or emotion card) necessitates a balanced heart. The alchemical process is depicted by the two cups in the center of the card, emphasizing that constant awareness of what needs to be balanced within The Fool is required, and that feelings must be addressed and expressed.

The Temperance card carries the unmistakable meaning of healthy and effective relationships, which are accomplished when the people involved are willing to compromise and cooperate. To maintain balance, fluidity and flexibility are required. The Temperance card's message is one of moderation.

Furthermore, since the angel is a heavenly figure, not an earthly one, Temperance implies heavenly intervention that "magically" generates the ultimate result of keeping this balance; life will flow with ease and grace once balance is maintained, ensuring a serene and joyful life. When the Temperance card appears in a reading, it is time for communicating sentiments rather than suppressing them. Truthful negotiations,

by forgiving differences, will end conflict.

Upright: If this card appears in a spread with The Lovers card, it suggests a lovely relationship, rekindling an old flame, or reaching an accord. It represents a balanced temperament, respite, moderation in behavior, and the possibility of reaching a settlement through negotiation. Also, a cooperative collaboration on a project or business with others, a conducive working environment if a new job is started, and the ability to compromise and adapt.

Modern Interpretation: Mediator, motivator, conductor, someone who brings harmony and balance. Promotion at work.

Reversed: Things out of balance. Quarrels and disagreements. Difficulty getting along with others. Restless competitiveness. Beware of doing too much, which results in scattering of your energy. Poor judgment. Bad health.

PHASE 3: FULFILLMENT (CARDS 15–22)

The Fool went through cycles of expansion and limitation in phase 2, prompting him to explore himself and reconcile evolving components of his personality. He was reminded that no matter how much he tries to control life, there will be periods of suspension to prepare him for the next cycle. To complete his metamorphosis, he must undergo comparable trials and lessons in phase 3, which are aimed to polish and reveal his true self as boundless consciousness in a human body.

The final stage entails addressing his dark shadow and releasing his human ego. "Death" was the first in a series of dramatic stages of growth in which The Fool was stripped of worldly pretensions in order to further clarify his individuality and how he connects with himself. After the repose of Temperance, The Fool is ready to deal with The Devil within him—a formidable character from his unconscious realm.

15—The Devil: Enslaved by the Ego

Despite The Fool's maturity, he is still vulnerable to his personal demons—materialistic compulsions and addictions. The Devil represents the shackles that prevent us from fully growing our spirit within a human form. Ignorance, untamed passion, obsessions, consumerism, fanaticism, excessive wrath, petty attachments, poor impulse control, and negative thinking are all examples of this bondage. Codependency, negative thoughts, self-imposed doubts, and anxiety can result from getting attached to desires of the ego without wisdom of the spirit within.

The card's image is strikingly similar to The Lovers card, in which the couple stand before us naked. However, this time they are chained by the Devil in darkness. It symbolizes being enslaved to the untamed "desires of the flesh." Moreover, their imprisonment is voluntary—they chose to be in this relationship; however, they can only be freed if they let go of the chains they placed around their necks—the unconscious and unbalanced (extreme) desires of the ego. They must acknowledge their shadow side in order to be free. Otherwise, the untransformed aspects of their personality will keep them imprisoned.

The Devil is depicted in the Tarot as a crouching goat on a pedestal. Typically, a man and a woman are chained to the pedestal. The Devil is commonly depicted with bat wings and horns, highlighting his dark nature. However, his hands are human, and they are also free, implying that the pair, or the duality in a person, chooses to be imprisoned by The Devil. It depicts the dark side of our personality, the aspects of ourselves that we are least proud of, or reject, preferring to bury them.

The Devil card does not reflect evil in

any way. It reflects the dark side of human beings—which is not evil, only in the dark. It forces The Fool to confront the murky, primeval side of himself that is inhibiting his transformation by releasing these aspects into the light. When facing the sun, the shadows fall behind. It symbolizes releasing oneself from voluntary confinement to unconscious or repressed desires. In a spread, this card represents an imbalanced attachment to a relationship that is not serving our highest good, or being imprisoned by our concerns and extreme desires.

As The Fool accepts his shadow, he develops tolerance and compassion for himself and others. Acceptance replaces prejudice and blame; he realizes that all humans are made up of a mix of good and bad, light and shadow. This realization allows him to be human and embrace his human limitations and feelings. The Devil represents the promise that when barriers are removed, enormous growth and progress can be accomplished.

Upright: False dependencies on material gains or desires. Buying friendship or love. Hidden fears, limitations, or restrictive circumstances. Often it indicates delays or difficulties in achieving one's goals. It also represents sexual attraction in the context of relationships—not love. Moreover, the inability to break from a relationship that does not make you happy, or in which you're being emotionally blackmailed. The Devil symbolizes destructive, obsessive behavior. A manipulative or egocentric personality. Abuse of power, money, sex, or personal charm, depending on where it falls in a spread. It can indicate depression if restrictive circumstances have been going on for a while.

Modern Interpretation: Emotional or sexual addiction, abusive violent personality, sex enslavement or trafficking.

Reversed: Obstacles or restrictions that have blocked your path are removed. You can see your way forward. Emotional shortcomings are overcome, and inner truth is uncovered. The ability to see through shallow, materialistic types.

16—The Tower: Sudden Destruction

After breaking free from the bonds of self-imposed limitations in his inner world, The Fool is struck by a bolt of lightning from The Tower to clear his external world. All that he has learned and gained is destroyed in order to restore balance on a new level. The moral of this lesson is that one has outgrown rigid structures in their life, and sudden, unexpected change is necessary to release limitations and establish new structures. This can turn out to be a blessing in disguise. Further transformation is taking place, where the inner and outer manifestation must be in harmony. If you like, the wisdom of this card is to help The Fool remain aware to modify the life he is creating, and in doing so fulfill his purpose.

The Tower highlights the need to break free from oppressive relationships or patterns and set the framework for redesigning one's life by erecting new structures. It takes The Devil's teachings to a new level. The Tower is about external, physical, and material loss or damage, and it annihilates the ego. Any assumptions and attitudes The Fool had about his previous world are demolished in order to make place for new ones. A new sense of freedom is arising to assist The Fool in developing a new identity—one of limitless possibilities.

The card depicts "heavenly" lightning striking the highest part of a tower, causing the building to collapse and dislodging the crown (symbolizing the dominion of spiritual laws over man's). Two figures, a man and a woman, signifying dualistic earthly life, fall to their deaths. The sky is filled with 22 sparks of light, representing the Tarot's 22 Major Arcana cards. The Tower is constructed of bricks on a high rock and signifies man's effort to govern physical reality and reach "heaven" by erecting tall constructions. The Tower card's symbology represents the destruction of The Fool's worldly illusions: false values and belief systems.

As a result of his encounters with Death and The Devil, he has acknowledged inner struggles, as well as the limitless possibilities he has at his disposal. The Devil has demonstrated the extent of his power, and Death has removed all sense of entitlement. The Tower will destroy remaining outdated assumptions. Divine lightning reaches the unconscious depths to dissipate dark energy and make way for fresh ideas. Change will be more painful if we are rigid and inflexible. The message is to adjust to the situation and move on.

Furthermore, The Tower is the only card in the deck that depicts a structure as its subject. The symbols on the other cards are cosmic bodies or figures, human or godlike. The structure represents society, and The Tower represents the totality of its laws and rules. The Fool must find out if his society's values relate to him. Change is the one constant in life, and this violent

image represents that.

Upright: Exhilarating change turns your world upside down. Changes can be disruptive, even violent, but are necessary, promising a positive outcome. Breakup of relationships or lifestyles; financial losses may be incurred; the picture is about going through an unstable phase. It denotes receiving shocking news, a sudden revelation, destruction of something corrupt. Depending on where it falls in a reading, it can indicate changes in health such as a stroke or heart attack, or loss of property, change of residence, loss of job, or separation of relationships.

Modern Interpretation: Sudden awakening, or a realization that will change your life. Electricity, digital communications and online news. Kundalini experience, where energy rises up the body to illuminate the mind.

Reversed: Disruptive and chaotic, need to accept upcoming changes. Not able to withstand pressure, nervous breakdown. You are advised to take less on board. The process of change has already begun; not going with the flow will result in stagnation and more problems. If you are repressing feelings of grief, rage, or disappointment, let them go and your life will soon improve.

17—The Star: Hope and Inspiration

The Fool sees The Star as a source of optimism and inspiration. It represents a new dawn after the dark tunnel of the inner world. He has learned that through flexibility, his resilience grew. Previous lessons taught him to let go of attachments and beliefs that are not conducive to growth. Continuous "purification" and rebirthing lessons prepared The Fool to receive his true wishes. He is now ready for further growth, illumination, and an easy-flowing life.

This is a cosmic card uniting "heaven and Earth." Kneeling beside a pool of water, naked, the lady of intuition and inspiration symbolizes the spiritual truth of thoughts and feelings. Her right foot is in the pool, signifying her connection to free-flowing feelings. Her left foot is planted on the ground, transmitting her healing intuitive abilities to the physical world. She pours life's waters from two cups, one in each hand (what card does this imagery remind you of?), implying that deeper purification of feelings is required to be inspired onto the right path. The sun is represented by the golden cup, while the moon is represented by the silver cup, symbolizing the equilibrium between yang and yin (activity and receptivity, respectively, logic and intuition). Seven silver stars shine above the naked maiden, symbolizing the seven cosmic bodies of classical astrology: Sun, Moon, Mercury, Venus, Mars, Jupiter and Saturn.

The sky is dominated by a huge, bright star with eight points. The star signifies the balance of opposing forces (Justice) in the cosmos (above as below). The soil around the pool appears to be fertile. A lone tree stands atop a mountain behind The Star, symbolizing the goal to be achieved by The Fool's mystical quest: to unite Spirit and matter. The tree represents being rooted to receive pure, exalted ideas and heavenly guidance (telepathy). The Star is linked to intuition, meditation, and nature's hidden aspects. The Star figure is inspired by the golden star in the heavens. She receives life energy from the golden star and transmits it to the Earth below, inspiring humankind.

Because The Star transmutes thoughts and emotions, it represents optimism, inspiration, and excellent health by presenting a heavenly figure on Earth. When a positive mindset is maintained, The Fool is connected to higher guidance, and "inspired" to realize (make real) a well-balanced, fulfilling life as well as a healthy body. This card exudes positivity and healing in every way. Although it is a night card, it is a bright and hopeful one symbolizing that no matter how dark and difficult times are, there is always hope for a new dawn and a brighter future. It's a message of hope, love, and spiritual guidance, as well as happiness and fulfillment.

Upright: This card represents optimism and ascension to higher spiritual levels through emotional experiences. Hope, wisdom, adventure, healing, a visionary, imagination, inspiration. This is a great time to reflect on what is important. There is hope for the future, and healing is possible. You are ready to both give and receive (heavenly) love.

Modern Interpretation: Professional athletes and performers who are focused and in control of their minds; people who are telepathic. Divine inspiration. Expansion of personalities and abilities. Telepathic communication (with different worlds).

Reversed: Pessimism and lack of judgment due to muddled feelings and thoughts (lack of inspiration), a sense of failure, losing hope, depression, limited vision, and doubts. Mistrusting inner

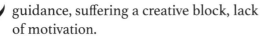

guidance, suffering a creative block, lack of motivation.

18—The Moon: Hidden Wisdom

The Fool's quest for enlightenment is due to end. He is still traveling in the celestial realm of The Moon, representing yet another cycle of change and development. He realizes that there is still much to learn from the "heavens." He had a brief but wonderful respite with The Star after the dark series of cards in the underworld, only to realize that the next card, The Moon, is another somber card. The Fool finds it difficult to see clearly while under the influence of the changing phases of the moon. Confusion, illusion, deception, and a lack of clarity are things The Fool learns to overcome. His mind is not at ease, because hidden influences are at work. The Moon symbolizes subconscious memories. To be totally aware, The Fool must awaken his subconscious mind and trust his innate senses.

The night image appears to be identical to The Star at first glance, but closer inspection reveals that it is not as tranquil as it appears. For instance, there is not a human figure in sight—only The Moon's changing faces and the darkness that ebbs and flows, representing mood swings. In the foreground, a crayfish, representing fears and anxieties pushing their way to the top of our awareness, is attempting to crawl out of the waters, only to be pushed back by the two animals on the shore, a dog and a wolf, who are howling at The Moon. The path between the two animals leads to the two pillars in the background, representing the duality of the unconscious and conscious. Bringing unconscious memories to the light leads to a path of awareness. It's like childhood worries reappearing in adulthood, still causing fear and anxiety, despite the fact that rationally they may not be recognized.

The crayfish will remain under water until The Fool recognizes that it must be allowed to rise and leave the murky waters. This pool is not the healing waters of The Star, but the muddled waters of repressed memories and thoughts.

The Moon represents the ephemeral, vague, and ambiguous character of emotions. She represents the unpredictable and uncontrollable surfacing of unconscious thoughts, memories, and intuition. These attributes must be transformed into wisdom to be assimilated into The Fool's personality. This is why The Moon usually indicates a fluctuating and changing phase in a reading. It denotes ambiguity, if not deception, and suggests that a solution to a problem might be found through the unconscious—namely dreams, rather than logic and reason.

The Moon is regarded as the mistress of the night, the womb where men go to rest, sleep, and dream. It rules the unconscious—the realm of dreams, desires, and imagination. Ideas or revelations received through the unconscious are difficult to explain or put into words logically. The Moon reigns over subtly inspired creativity, where bits of information are revealed over time, like the cycles of the Moon. If you like, a gestation period is necessary for the idea to grow. In this aspect, The Moon represents matters that are not yet revealed, secrets, and pregnancies—all of which will come to fruition. Once the idea takes shape, it will be revealed under the light of the Sun, or given birth to.

As The Fool transforms, the unconscious must be paid attention to. Dreams are likely to change as he becomes more self-aware, because dreams are the language of the unconscious mind. Once the business of the day winds down, and The Fool prepares to enter the womb of the night, the unconscious begins to release what it needs to bring into his awareness. At night, The Fool is not distracted by the demands of physical reality and can perceive the soft communication of the unconscious. This card is also about unifying the conscious and unconscious, implying that we are likely to suffer mood swings or irksome anxiety if subconscious memories and beliefs are not worked with.

Upright: The Moon represents darkness, confusion, and a lack of clarity. However, as Moon cycles change, the truth will be revealed through intuition or dreams. Psychic impressions, information from dreams. Unexpected change in a situation or feelings. Need for sleep. Rely on self. Harnessed imagination producing creative output. This card indicates hidden issues and anxieties, and guidance through dreams.

Reversed: Self-deception and self-destruction phase due to being misled by false intuition or illusion. Fear of unknown, hallucinations, not seeing problems in true light. Deception from friends. Negative illusions. Practical considerations take precedence over intuition or hunches. Do not take risks. Instead, work with the facts until the turmoil is over. Do not be concerned if you suspect someone is working behind your back. Their plans will be exposed soon. Could also indicate miscarriage or false pregnancy, depending on the other cards in the spread.

19—The Sun: Success, Prosperity, and Joy

After emerging from the light of The Moon, The Fool basks in the radiance of The Sun. The cobwebs of confusion and uncertainty dissolve as The Sun rises above The Fool. He experiences renewed energy and drive as well as clarity of thought. His ideas will come to fruition under The Sun, which promises a new cycle of renewal, success, and happiness. The Fool returns to the faith and openness of a child; his confidence is renewed. Success and expansion have come because of his efforts in overcoming the challenges of this transformational process.

The Sun has a longer cycle than the Moon, which was depicted in the preceding card. This represents long-term plans and ambitions that will require more time to be realized. It also represents the near future rather than the immediate future. However, we see The Fool in his child-like form, happily and effortlessly riding a white horse without holding the reins. This symbolizes the result of implementing the spiritual enlightenment he achieved in the material world and effortless success, as the sunflowers on the wall behind him grow toward The Sun. He is carrying a crimson banner, suggesting renewed zeal and optimism. The rising sun in the blue sky sends her warmth to the sunflowers on the wall, which represent not only renewed energy but also vitality, longevity, endless creative flow, sexual drive, and vigor.

The message of the card appears to be that in the mystical journey for unity with spiritual understanding, innocence and purity are essential; efforts are rewarded by success and abundant creative energy.

Upright: This is one of the Tarot's most cheerful cards. In a reading, it represents joy, happiness, and success in material gain, as well as good health. It also suggests that now is the time to explore your creativity and put into action any projects that desire to grow in the future. Now is the time for expansion and success. Happiness, vitality. Better finances, enjoying work and good health are indicated when The Sun appears in a reading.

Moreover, it indicates a person with great talent and skills that will be recognized. And also, the possibility of moving to a warm country, or significant meetings connected with overseas. Moreover, successful happy marriages or committed relationships, and the birth of a child are indicated. This is the start of a rewarding cycle in your life, and the best time to take advantage of opportunities. It is an invitation to live life to the fullest.

Reversed: The Sun reversed is never a bad card, but it has fewer positive qualities than when it appears upright in a reading. It implies that right now your future does not look as bright as it can be, or that you are not trying as hard as you can to achieve the success you desire. It can symbolize overconfidence, vanity, and arrogance that blocks success, depending on the overall spread. Also, difficulties in partnerships, or worries about children can be implied—look for neighboring cards.

20—Judgment:
Total Transformation

Every action we take has long-term ramifications. After being stripped of his ego (Death) and his possessions (Tower), The Fool is ready to be reborn to a new beginning, his true and larger purpose. He is now able to welcome the trumpet of Judgment, which calls for spiritual rebirth and healing of his psyche, after being re-energized by the Sun's light. He goes through a transformation and is resurrected as his true self. This card reflects The Fool's final evaluation regarding his development, wisdom, and maturity.

The image of the Judgment card conjures up the most dreadful vision of judgment day. To the sound of the trumpet calling them to a better (way of) life, graves open and bodies emerge, raising their hands toward the angel above. This card is also known as The Resurrection or The Angel in different Tarot decks. The picture of the dead rising represents an expected new cycle beginning as the old one comes to an end. The hands of the resurrected are raised in joy at the next cycle, indicating relief at shedding their worldly possessions and the limiting hang-ups of material personality—the final death of the past.

Extremes are evaluated. Excessive arrogance, like self-deprecation, must be brought into balance to ascend to the higher wisdom of living. The resurrected dead are undergoing spiritual rebirth. Judgment represents reaping what we have sown. The Fool must accept responsibility for the outcomes of the decisions he made along the Tarot journey. This is one of life's most important lessons: life is primarily shaped by the decisions we make, and we live with the consequences of our decisions.

Notice the snow-topped mountains on the horizon, indicating the ultimate spiritual goal: enlightenment. This is not a card of ending, for the child in the foreground faces the mountains in the background, signifying that he is looking forward to the future. Although the card looks ominous, Judgment marks the end of a karmic cycle, indicates a "clean slate," and sends a message: *"You have paid your dues; it's a time of rejoicing and renewal."* Like the child in The Sun card, this child, the resurrected Fool, embraces the wisdom to come.

Upright: It denotes an inescapable positive shift, even though it appears to be unfavorable. Reward for past effort, re-evaluation, responsibility, outcome, resolution, acceptance. New lease on life, transformation, major decisions, changes, healing has taken place. Spiritual awakening. Death of old self. Death of previous lifestyle.

Reversed: Stagnation, refusal to accept change. Delays in completion, success or achievement, overdue awakening—the old ways are no longer working for you.

21—The World: Total Integration

This is the final stage of The Fool's development. The Fool floats like a fetus amidst the now-circling oval wreath in The World. This is the concluding card of The Fool's adventure. In contrast to his image as The Fool, card zero, the small wreath over his hat at the beginning expanded to the large wreath he floats in, implying mystical existence. He succeeded in uniting his dualistic nature, having stripped himself of false identities and ego personalities. The purple ribbon of spiritual wisdom covers his genitals, implying that his instinctive desire no longer controls him. Now he has a female appearance, similar to the figure in the Star card, representing his truthful (naked) non-dualistic nature, where male and female are united. Attaining equilibrium is symbolized by the two white wands the figure is holding and the four symbols at each corner of the image, where number 4 represents stability. He has successfully attained this state.

The four corner figures represent the four elements and four seasons. We have a complete circle in which all the minor cycles are linked to this long cycle of renewal. The four seasons also indicate that The Fool is aware of nature's changing cycles, and of how other events are governed by cycles too. They represent the four aspects of his nature as a man, which he is now in command of: personality, instincts, and desires, as well as his spiritual nature. The earthly head of a man in the clouds depicts winter and air elements, both symbolizing the personality. The bull in the bottom left-hand corner represents spring and the earth element, denoting earthly desires and fertility. The lion represents summer and the element of fire, denoting primal instincts; and the eagle represents autumn and the element of water, signifying his spiritual nature.

In a reading, The World denotes the successful completion of a period of achievement and the beginning of a cycle of harmony and fulfillment. The Fool has totally blended with nature and the cosmos. He is one with all. The World symbolizes The Fool's past experiences, all of life's cycles, including beginnings and endings, losses and gains, separation and unification. He has bridged the gap between his spiritual and human self, transcending the duality of human nature. The end of these transformative cycles is announced by the trumpet of Judgment. The Fool has gained wisdom through understanding the various stages of the challenges he encountered. Actualization of the self is now complete. Fulfillment and wholeness bring joy that exceeds that of The Sun. The World is his!

However, the cycles of life are not over. The World marks the beginning of a new cycle, presenting The Fool as a fetus who is about to be born—albeit on a different level.

Upright: In a reading, this card denotes the completion of a significant cycle or stage of life. Achievement and recognition are due. It signifies success, fame, harmonious living, fulfillment, receiving an award, or the next cycle of expansion. It is time to celebrate and embrace recognition. It also announces a significant promotion or beneficial job change.

Modern Interpretation: Performing on stage, publishing, successful art exhibit, expanded online presence, extensive travel, intelligent wisdom, further expansion of awareness and self-mastery.

Reversed: Like The Sun card, The World reversed is never a bad omen. However, it denotes stagnation, or refusal to accept acknowledgments or expansion, delays in completion, success, or achievement.

CHAPTER THREE

GETTING TO KNOW THE TAROT

Having shared the journey of The Fool so far, you might be aware of the repeated themes, imagery, and symbols in the Tarot. Mountains, for example, can represent major challenges, whereas rocks or hills can represent modest ones. Animals frequently represent instincts, animal nature, or desires. Water is a universal symbol for feelings and emotions. As you review the cards, look at the pictures with water in them; notice how water is expressed on each card, as well as the meaning conveyed. Birds represent ideas as well as spiritual goals. And of course the colors used in the Tarot also have meaning.

Below are highlights of some significant symbols and colors. You might find this helpful before you choose a Tarot deck. Images trigger the imagination and express what words cannot. Imagination sparks intuition. As you interact with several decks or images, you will get to know which deck works for you.

Tarot Themes

The Tarot symbolizes cycles of development that are transformative and alchemical in nature. They are designed to continuously "recycle" and purify anything that holds us back from expressing our true infinite and creative nature. To gain the necessary wisdom to create a fulfilling life, it is essential to fine-tune the human instrument, shedding any false desires or attachments that distract you from achieving what is possible. Fulfillment comes through maintaining balance and reconciling conflicts within the self, as well as harmonizing with the exterior world.

The Tarot imparts a great deal of knowledge, expressed as images; that is why symbols are important. Nowadays, there are myriad themes in the Tarot decks. However, whichever deck you choose to work with, notice which symbols are featured and what they trigger in you. In this book, the Rider-Waite-Smith deck is chosen for the abundance of symbols to help you develop your intuition.

COLORS

Red: Earthly desires, creative drive, sensual and sexual cravings, instincts, power, and authority are all represented by red. Red represents blood, life, desire, and the planet Mars. It symbolizes vitality, strength, energy, sex, passion, and a healthy body. It denotes the yang aspect of doing, accomplishing, building, and

Tarot
Rider Waite
1910

Illustrated
Pamela Colman Smith

Figure II The Major Arcana

producing. They have a strong presence in The Magician, The Emperor, The Hierophant, and Justice. The majority of these figures symbolize the male side, which leads, controls, constructs, and has power or authority. It is frequently balanced with white.

White: Spiritual understanding attained through self-awareness. It symbolizes illumination, daylight, joy, openness, and enlightenment. Cards with white convey heavenly involvement in the material world, emphasizing the importance of uniting Spirit and materialism, or

transmuting opposites to create an ideal "heavenly" outcome.

Yellow: Intellectual wisdom or mind mastery. It appears as the background behind The Fool, The Magician, The Empress, The Lovers, The Chariot, and Strength. In The Tower, the bolt of lightning represents waking up or enlightening the intellect. Yellow is also the prominent color of the major star in The Star card, The Moon, and The Sun, as well as the hair color of the female characters and the Judgment card's angel.

Orange: This color is not immediately obvious, but it is significant, continuously alluding to controlling man's sexual desires. It is also the color of sensuality and physical pleasures.

Blue: Blue represents the color of The Moon. It signifies the goddess inside, the feminine aspect of intuition, emotions, inner life, and psychic ability. Moreover, perceiving inspirational wisdom through dreams, psychic abilities, the natural cycles of rest needed by man—night-time, where imagination and intuition peak and the mind receives knowledge from the heavens. There is a healing, soft quality to blue.

Purple: Purple is used mindfully in the Tarot. It is the traditional color of royalty; it denotes nobility, pride, justice, and the upper order of spiritual authorities. We notice it twice: once in the shawl of The Lovers' angel, embracing the couple with heavenly wisdom; and again, as the ribbon or sash spiraling around The World card's figure, signifying that spiritual wisdom is the goal of earthly endeavors.

Gray: Gray is usually the color of storm clouds, mourning, bereavement, sadness, or despair. In the Tarot, it reflects wisdom gained by experience, and reconciliation.

It symbolizes spiritual wisdom manifested, as seen in the figure of The Hermit. It also indicates that spiritual metamorphosis is taking place in the body or skin color of the Sun figure, as well as in the resurrected people in the Judgment card.

Green: Green represents vegetation and a rich, bountiful existence, as well as hope, serenity, fertility, growth, safety, security, health, youth, and abundant life force.

Black: Black is like a stop sign that says, "Halt and pay attention!" It balances white (Spirit) and appears whenever the duality theme is represented.

NATURE & LANDSCAPES

Most Major Arcana cards represent a natural scene, emphasizing that the goal is to live a better life on Earth—it is a direct relationship to earthly existence, indicating the visible effect of man's actions.

Landscapes: The terrain often depicts a season, which provides further information. Consider the landscape of the figure or event taking place—as in the Minor cards—when looking at a Tarot card. The landscape will frequently tell you whether it is the season of development and expansion (spring), joy and happiness (summer), deliberate strategy (fall), or tangible results (winter). They illustrate the seasonal cycles that govern nature and, as a result, govern man's actions.

Nature represents that there is a proper time to act, based on the "seasonal" cycle. It also demonstrates the effect of our labor. In other words, we reap what we sow. The latter is the key to transformation.

Also consider the age of the figure in the card in relation to the landscape around it. Note what age they are and how are they acting. In the Five of Wands, although the figures are all holding Wands, the terrain is arid and not smooth, reflecting trouble or conflict. They are young and fighting—as youths do, when wisdom is lacking! You will find a correlation between these elements in the illustration, particularly in the Minor Arcana, where we see the developmental stages of The Fool's four personality aspects as he grows: his body and ideas, emotions, thoughts, and the results of his actions.

Water: Whereas the soil element (of landscapes) is solid (fixed) and depicts the results of actions, water is fluid and depicts emotions and sentiments. It represents a fluid part of human nature that humans must balance in order to progress

to the next stage of their evolution. What is beneath the waters—the subconscious—is also significant. Notice whether the waters are stagnant or flowing, clear or cloudy, choppy or calm. All of these hint at a person's mental state.

Mountains: Significant goals are symbolized by mountains, lesser ones by hills. They are often in the background, as a goal to be attained by The Fool—the purpose of the passage or lesson he must overcome, if you like. Mountains can snow-topped, indicating the ultimate objective of growth; or nearby, denoting a goal that can be reached. Mountaintops covered with snow may represent a long-term spiritual goal as well. It is these details that make the Tarot an effective visual tool to trigger the imagination and intuition of the reader.

Gardens, forests, and vegetation: Another motif in the Tarot is growing nature, which is especially evident in the Minor cards that depict the nature of each element. Nature sets the scene for each Tarot character. It explains the figure's impact, skills, and abilities, or the lesson behind that stage of personal development.

Cards in the Major Arcana that lack flora, fruits or vegetation represent

personal or spiritual growth. The absence of nature allows the viewer to focus on the nature of the card itself, or the significance of this stage of development or transformation.

Flowers: Three flowers only are depicted in the Rider-Waite-Colman deck: roses, lilies, and sunflowers. Pomegranates and grapes (particularity in the Pentacles suit), as fruits, are also featured, symbolizing fertility and wealth, respectively.

Roses are often red, symbolizing passion, drive, initiation of inspired ideas, and an abundance of creativity (the potential). White lilies depict a spiritual aspect to a situation, pure emotion, or the nature of the figure depicted in the card, symbolizing that creative ideas are inspired by Spirit. Often, they are small details on flower garlands, or in the foreground of a card's illustration, such as The Magician, where red roses and white lilies together symbolize the balance of thought and desire, or head and heart.

OBJECTS

Objects that a figure holds or uses have significance, adding depth to the meaning of the card. For example, crowns depict authority, a degree of mastery, and the

ability to govern and lead. Below are some of the notable objects in the Tarot.

Robes: Robes wrap a figure in its prominent traits and attributes, completing their significance and what each card represents. To visually convey these features, much detail has gone into the robes. Pay attention to what the figures are wearing not in terms of fashion, but rather their "lifestyle." Their clothing would reflect what the figures had accomplished, who they are, and what aspects of human personality they represent.

The Queen of Swords, for example, is wearing a blue cloak with clouds, in contrast to her gown, which is a dull gray color (the mind is always in connection with Spirit and needs to be transformed or kept in check) with orange trim. What do you believe this imagery represents?

Her crown and the sword in her hand indicate that she is the Queen of Swords. Her cape, however, indicates that she rules over the domain of the mind, as represented by the shifting or floating clouds against the blue sky; and the orange trim indicates that, contrary to her stern facial expression, she does feel compassion, has feelings, and enjoys pleasures or sensuality (in measure, however). There is a stream behind her throne, which adds an aspect of sentiment and intuition to this queen, but her decision is to be attentive, to rule fairly by reason, but to be ready to act whenever necessary.

Crown: The crown represents a figure's "crowning" skill or ability—the source of their capacity, skill, drive, or sphere of sovereignty. The Crown symbolizes the mind's sovereignty of matter. It is also the center of receiving inspiration from Spirit. In the Tarot, there are at least 17 crowns, and no two are alike. Each one is decorated with objects. For example, the crown on The Tower card signifies human rule or triumph over the Earth, as well as worldly achievement. The Tower is located on a high mountaintop, which serves as another emblem for the world's kingdoms. The lightning strikes the crown, a symbol of human glory or, indeed, arrogance, and it crashes back to Earth, along with the people. What humans establish, believing it to be permanent, turns out to be transient.

Other crowns are presented as laurel wreaths, normally if the event depicted shows a triumph, in a Minor cycle, over a great challenge. Usually, the authority of the figure depicted is less than that of a King or Queen—for example, the Six of Wands, or the female in The Lovers

card, the Strength card, and the happily dancing maidens of the Three of Cups. Laurel wreaths or garlands as crowns tend to have a celebratory feel, rather than a Major achievement or authority (although, in the case of Strength, her crown is further enforced by the infinity sign over her head, indicating infinite possibilities of channeling spirit energy for beneficial use on Earth).

Crowns are decorated with flowers, reflecting the drive or vigor of the monarch, and their wealth and abundance if they are bejeweled (The Emperor, Justice). Sometimes they have shapes on them as well, like the crown of Justice (a square) or the illuminated crown of Temperance (a circle and a dot). Other crowns are elaborate, denoting how powerful the figure is over his or her domain, such as in The High Priestess's moon crown, the intricate starry crown of The Empress, the layered crown of The Hierophant reaching toward the sky, and The Chariot's crown, adorned with a big yellow star that combines logic and intuition.

However, two crowns are most intriguing: the one atop the Ace of Swords, and the one on the head of the figure in The Four of Pentacles. Both are Minor cards, which are not Court Cards. The first symbolizes mastery of mind over actions;

the other symbolizes mastery of tangible manifestations of money—both achieved through balance.

Halo: The Hanged Man and Temperance are two figures with halos in the Major Arcana; both signify that an illuminated mind has been achieved. The first by pausing and (literally) seeing things from a different perspective, and the second implying that an illuminated mind (through inspiration, since the figure is an angel) can resolve any conflict. Its image in the Tarot is not confined to a heavenly figure with a halo, but rather to attaining wisdom and illumination (enlightenment). The only other Minor Arcana cards portraying a halo are the Seven of Cups and the Ten of Cups, where the cups are illuminated to attract attention, and announce something—a solution or a result.

Homes or castles: Aside from the obvious, dwellings signify earthly accomplishments. A castle is the home of Minor card Kings and Queens who have mastered their element or personality aspect. As a result, the size and prominence of a castle are important. It represents one's achievements—the tangible result of the unification of dualities inside oneself.

IMAGE FORMATION

Foregrounds and backgrounds: Foregrounds tend to focus on the main message of the card, and backgrounds on the secondary influence or transformation taking place. The two cards that seem to be symmetrical on formation are The Wheel of Fortune and The World, where a central circular form is balanced by four smaller outer symbols in each corner. Balanced aspects (in the background) highlight the result of the central symbol in the foreground. Overleaf there is a table highlighting possible interpretations of the Major cards' images.

DEVELOPMENTAL CYCLES

The four elemental suits of the Minor Arcana illustrate the evolving facets of The Fool's personality. They represent The Fool progressing from a Page to a King, who "rules" through achieving his full potential and mastering his ego personality. The four Minor Arcana suits reflect the four stages of personality development as follows:

Wands: Wands represent The Fool taking initiatives to forge his own way, developing and implementing his ideas and projects while listening to spiritual guidance. In other words, he is paying attention to, or becoming aware of, what inspires him. He is trusting himself, his wisdom and potential, despite his lack of experience or skills.

Cups: Cups symbolize The Fool's emotional growth through forging alliances and partnerships. He falls in love, trusts others, and collaborates with them. He learns to distinguish between different emotions, which arise from attachments, upsetting his balance. But his true feelings, characterized by balance and harmony leading to growth, enable him to fulfill his passions and identify the right romantic and business partners. Despite the possibility of disappointment, The Fool learns to reflect, confront his truth, and move in a new direction toward his goal. And when he trusts without being attached to false expectations, his wishes come true, as if by magic.

Swords: The Fool discovers how emotions affect the mind and how his mentality affects his feelings. After taking initiative and learning to trust his genuine sentiments, he learns that balancing or regular adjustment of his thoughts is essential to arriving at the best decisions. He discovers that growth is a never-ending

process, and that if he wants to attain tangible outcomes, he must acknowledge and overcome unconscious anxieties. His ultimate lesson is that if he does not decide, he risks becoming trapped by fears and anxieties. His perception of a situation is sometimes far worse than the actuality of it. The upshot of developing a flexible intellect is a constructive decision-making process that yields positive results. In the next suit, he learns to accept responsibility for his decisions.

Pentacles: Pentacles reflect the completion of The Fool's individuation, and emotional and mental processes. Following his own path requires him to be responsible for his financial independence by expressing his potential creativity, ability, and skills. The four suits, or aspects of personality, work together simultaneously. Each Minor Arcana suit has an impact on the others, illustrating the complexities of maturity. If The Fool does not collaborate, or plan expansion, or have the right mind-set, no tangible results will be achieved. And if his efforts are not consistent, revised, and flexible, no success will be achieved. The results symbolized by the Pentacles Minor Arcana are experienced in the material world. They are not feelings or thoughts, but present the consequences of current

CARD	NUMBER	FOREGROUND SYMBOL	FOREGROUND KEYWORDS
THE FOOL	0	White dog	Innocence, intention
THE MAGICIAN	1	Red roses and white lilies	Creativity and drive
THE HIGH PRIESTESS	2	New moon, flowy robes	Psychic, moody, fluid state, uncertain
THE EMPRESS	3	Dried corn sheaf	Germination, potential, fertility
THE EMPEROR	4	Stone throne	Structure
THE HIEROPHANT	5	Two people	Advice
THE LOVERS	6	Two people	Two people, relationship
THE CHARIOT	7	Two lions	Balancing
JUSTICE	8	White foot	Justice on Earth
THE HERMIT	9	Snow	Height of spiritual wisdom
WHEEL OF FORTUNE	10	A symbol in each corner	Balance
STRENGTH	11	Lion	Primal desires
THE HANGED MAN	12	Illuminated head	Enlightenment
DEATH	13	Dead king, arid land	Death
TEMPERANCE	14	Water	Emotions
THE DEVIL	15	Chained couple	Imprisonment
THE TOWER	16	High rock/mountain	Big achievement
THE STAR	17	Water	Emotions
THE MOON	18	Crayfish crawling	Trying to get out
THE SUN	19	Child on a horse	Happy
JUDGMENT	20	Dead rising from graves	Resurrections
THE WORLD	21	Symmetrical	A symbol in each corner

Figure 12 Foreground and background image formation of the Major Arcana

CARD *(continued)*	NUMBER	BACKGROUND SYMBOL	BACKGROUND KEYWORDS
THE FOOL	0	Snow-topped mountains	Objective, spiritual enlightenment
THE MAGICIAN	1	Red rose vine	Successful achievement
THE HIGH PRIESTESS	2	Pomegranate veil	Fertility, balanced intuition
THE EMPRESS	3	Growing forest	Success
THE EMPEROR	4	Stone throne	Structure
THE HIEROPHANT	5	Crown, two pillars	Higher wisdom
THE LOVERS	6	Angel	Balance
THE CHARIOT	7	Starry canopy & crown	Inspirational victory
JUSTICE	8	Purple veil	Truth to be revealed (consider all aspects)
THE HERMIT	9	Gray	Spiritual transformation
WHEEL OF FORTUNE	10	Circular object	Cycle
STRENGTH	11	Woman in white	Spiritual feminine influence
THE HANGED MAN	12	Tree trunk with leaves	Growth
DEATH	13	Water and life growing	Continuity
TEMPERANCE	14	Wings	Balance
THE DEVIL	15	Bat wings, reversed pentacle	Out of balance
THE TOWER	16	Bolt of lightning	Sudden
THE STAR	17	Stars	Inspiration
THE MOON	18	Moon faces	Change in progress
THE SUN	19	Sun	Joy
JUDGMENT	20	Trumpet	Call
THE WORLD	21	Egg-shaped wreath	Cycle

emotional and mental states. In other words, they manifest reality, where The Fool has to learn to be responsible for his own growth.

The table on pages 92-3 summarizes the essence of each of the developmental cycles as they are expressed in the Minor Arcana suits. When you first start interpreting Tarot readings, you can refer to it for guidance.

Preparing Yourself for a Reading

TAPPING INTO YOUR INTUITION

By practicing, you will improve your reading skills. You, like our hero, The Fool, are embarking on a psychic adventure. But don't worry; no one is judging you, so please don't judge yourself. It inhibits your imagination—the very thing Tarot helps enhance.

Set aside some time when you are not going to be distracted. Take a few deep breaths and let go of the day's events as well as any expectations you may have placed on your abilities. You can also light

a tea-light candle and focus your attention for a few moments on the flickering flame. Start this "infinity exercise" by holding your pen or pencil steady and relaxed:

1. If you have a Tarot journal, draw an infinity figure at the back of it, using your dominant hand.

2. Go over it as closely as you can to the original outline you drew, until you're comfortable with it and it flows without restraining your focus.

3. Now, using your weaker hand, trace over that outline, maintaining as much as possible the original shape. It may seem awkward at first, but that's to be expected. This simple "coordination" exercise is training the brain, so be patient as one side of your brain learns to do what the other side normally does.

4. When you feel comfortable using your other hand, hold the pen with both hands and go over your infinity figure, staying close to the previously drawn outline. The objective here is NOT speed, but relaxed, mindful focus.

5. Repeat each step about ten times, or until it flows smoothly.

The infinity exercise improves intuition and allows the hemispheres of the brain to work in unison.

MAKING A START

The easiest way to learn to use the Tarot is to do so as you get to know and trust the cards—especially before you learn any spreads, meanings, or interpretations. Your initial reactions are important in determining what each card represents to you. It helps you build a connection with them, contributing to the knowledge you will gain later.

Be brave, and start investigating right now by doing readings for yourself, even if they are about mundane issues. It is a good chance to get your cards used to being shuffled by your hands and to put your energy into them—especially if others will be handling your deck as well. Simply ask direct questions while you shuffle, and then choose one card from the entire deck. Place the chosen card in front of you and reflect on the image as an artistic expression.

You can follow the five steps below to help build your routine or approach:

1. Ask one question.

2. Write down your observations in your Tarot journal, and date your entries.

3. Dating your entries allows you to reflect on significant milestones that shape your Tarot learning experience.

4. Describe the most obvious remarks first. This method grounds your intuition in logic. Once you have done that, your creativity will flow easily and you will be able to balance reasoning and intuition (as The Chariot), conquering the task at hand.

5. Establishing this technique helps you weave a story around any insights you receive when using several cards in a single spread. Over time, your readings will have context as well as relevance and accuracy.

Regarding Step 4, make your descriptions visual—doodle if you like—and poetic to stimulate your imagination. What colors and images on the card appeal to you? What symbolic meaning does that color bring to mind? If the section on colors earlier in this chapter resonates with your sensibilities, refer back to it for more inspiration. Begin by silently speaking the words to yourself, taking your time with this process.

Write each sentence mindfully, focusing on the words that signify something to you, and relate them to your life. If you have an image of a figure, for example, describe who he or she is, who they remind you of, what they are wearing, the expression on their face, and whether it brings back a memory. What sort of throne are they sitting on? Does it remind you of someone's attitude? Are there any natural factors such as breezes, clouds, or vegetation in the image? Are there other objects in the image? If so, what is the purpose of those objects? And so on. Keep writing and describing what you see, and relating it to your experiences, impressions or memories. Don't hurry this process.

Here are a few tips that can stimulate writing descriptions in your journal entry:

- Write longhand (do not type). This allows brain waves to slow down and connect more deeply with the creative hemisphere of the brain.
- Do not stop writing. If you doubt yourself, or hesitate, you will bring yourself out of this "meditative" state; that might interrupt your imagination and obstruct your intuition from unfolding. If you run out of things to describe, write something like this: "I am looking at the image of the Tower... I am breathing deeply and I am relaxed, just gazing at this image. What I see is this... I do not know if the Tower is crumbling, but I can see that people are falling off..." etc.
- Do not take your pen off the paper. Doodle, write abstract words that come to mind, but keep your pen on the paper. It will build confidence, teach you to trust your intuition, and train you to allow information to flow.
- You will know when to stop writing. Insights have a way of revealing themselves!

Your journal entries can look something like this:

Question: *"What am I going to learn about myself today through you?"*

Card Selected: The Tower

Scene of a tower crumbling down.

Type: Major card.

Factual description:
It is dark (night).
There is a bolt of lightning.
Crown knocked off.
People falling off a cliff.

My insights: *"Something happened all of a sudden, as quick as a bolt of lightning. It comes as a surprise in the middle of the night. There will be ramifications because the result of this is that the Tower is totally destroyed, and people are falling off. Change is (probably) permanent. I can relate to this because it reminds me of a time when I was taken by surprise. I feel that what I took for granted in the past was like that crown I wore on my head. Suddenly my crown was knocked off, and I was not prepared. My world was shaken, and it took me time to recover. What I believed to be true was suddenly destroyed, like this tower. I have a challenge to conquer. Maybe it is a belief I hold, since the crown is what I noticed most, and a crown is worn on my head. The belief I have in my head needs to be destroyed because it is false, not true, and will be destroyed suddenly. If I am not aware of this, I might repeat an old memory. I am tired of repeating the past, so must therefore change something about my false belief or view of myself or my life. I feel uneasy, maybe because I need to let go and not repeat the past... The belief I have to change is ... And I need to build a new view regarding my view of ... There is no going back."*

Your mind relaxes as you begin to describe the facts about the card's image and what first struck you about the card: whether it was an image, a figure, a symbol or a color. Since what you're describing is logical and factual, your inhibitions or doubts will move out of the way. Soon enough, you will begin to connect with your imagination as you continue to write without pausing or thinking. And your intuition will flow freely with new insights. If you wish, you can shuffle again, asking the next (common-sense) question: *"What is holding me back?"* Draw a card randomly and start another entry in your Tarot journal to intuit what the card means to you in relation to the question you first asked.

By now, your creative juices are probably still flowing, and you're eager to find out what you can do to help you make that change, and unblock what you uncovered in Card 2. Shuffle your cards once more, asking, *"What can support me in overcoming this challenge?"* Start another entry and see what insights you receive from your new deck. Next, look at the three cards you selected randomly, which are laid out in front of you. Start a new Tarot journal entry, and describe what you laid out, perhaps something like this:

Card 1 Question: *"What am I going to learn about myself today through you?"*

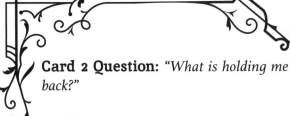

Card 2 Question: *"What is holding me back?"*

Card 3 Question: *"What can support me in overcoming this challenge?"*

Congratulations! You have designed your first three-card spread and interpreted your first card reading! You will find more details on how to cast spreads in the next chapter.

Hopefully this section has inspired you to take a leap into the unknown and start your unique Tarot adventure. Remember, practice makes perfect. Experience is more valuable than information. Your Tarot experience helps you build a strong bond with the cards and enjoy a fluent and coherent conversation. You start to detect patterns and card combinations that speak to you, making your reading profoundly precise. When you first start Tarot readings, it is natural to refer to your Tarot journal or to this book. However, as your connection deepens, you will be referring less to other interpretations and more to your own.

What a Tarot Reading Is

In the next chapter, some Tarot spreads will be explored to help you start reading the cards. Practice will let you know which ones to use and when.

A Tarot reading consists of three components:
- You, the reader, and your psychic talent.
- The reader's understanding of each card's symbology and significance.
- The reader's ability to interpret the significance of a combination of three or more cards in a spread.

You play an important role in what makes a great and enlightening reading. The more self-aware you are, and the more you work on improving and evolving as a person, the more meaningful your readings will be. Here are seven pointers to help you create clear guidance:

1. Establish a routine: create and stick to a routine before and after using the cards. Routine is the energetic structure that holds and supports the steady development of your intuition.

2. Adopt an "inspire and empower" attitude (this is also a core value of the author). Whether in your psychic development or your Tarot readings, do not be spooked by, or look for, phenomena or drama. Go steadily and confidently. When reading for other people, try not to inject fear or doubt into their mind. Tarot is about empowerment, not woo-woo. So intend to stay authentic and ethical. You are a vessel for guidance.

3. Look after your own well-being. Psychic work can be draining and affect your health negatively. Center yourself, and clear and recharge before and after a session. Drink plenty of water, eat healthily, and get restful sleep. Human beings are walking batteries; water will help circulate, clear, and maintain a steady energy flow.

4. Keep up your Tarot journal: your journal is the "gatekeeper" of your learning and psychic journey.

5. Stop looking and start using what you've learned about the Tarot. Your learning journey has already begun; now plan to continue. Use the Tarot as much as you need to in order to understand your life's process and enhance your progress. When an answer is not clearly presented, especially one you do not want to confront, stop and check later, when you are more settled. When you start influencing the cards with your expectations, you lose your clarity and objectivity. And, of course, you miss out on learning the lesson behind your situation.

6. Hold your ego under control (like The Chariot) and stay true to yourself; the accuracy of a reading is dependent on your ability to keep an open mind and maintain your integrity with the Tarot. Before you start, take deep breaths, or meditate, and state your affirmation before you start shuffling the cards.

7. Hold yourself accountable; it is empowering, as you learned from The Fool's journey. Whenever you're not sure how to interpret a reading, simply ask yourself, *"What does this card mean?"* or *"What is it showing me?"* and your intuition will guide you. When you are reading for other people, simply say, *"I'm not sure what this indicates,"* without fear of losing credibility. You will jeopardize your integrity if you make up an interpretation or provide a bad one.

TAROT SPREADS

Tarot readings require laying out three or more cards or "spreading" them according to a template or a designated layout where each position is preassigned a meaning. Insight into a straightforward issue or question is better suited to simpler spreads, such as a one-, two- or three-card spread. They are also ideal spreads to ease a novice into conducting a reading, and preparing for more complex spreads. The latter provides more extensive insights, spanning numerous layers and covering a longer period of time. Complex spreads also require multiple cards, and often combine Major and Minor cards. More complexity, more depth of insight!

A reading will provide more layers of interpretation and depth of information the more complicated a spread is. Take your time in getting to know the Major cards well, because they're the foundation of self-awareness and life direction. Minor cards are also important, but as you learned, they provide insights into everyday events and are best used to provide additional individualized insights, if you like, after having laid the Major cards. You will learn about and practice with some practical spreads in the next chapter. Try your hand at using each spread, and determine which one to use, and for which type

of reading. As with most readers, you will inevitably have two or three favorites. First, let's look at "The Interview Spread" before we conclude this chapter on connecting with your new cards.

You do not have to be a seasoned Tarot reader to create your own spreads. In truth, it is an excellent technique to quickly grasp what the Tarot is. Even if you haven't memorized the meanings, you'll be able to understand the cards almost immediately. Practicing laying cards according to Tarot spreads gets you to the essence of Tarot learning. Furthermore, the spread you create is always appropriate for your needs.

Moreover, because there are so many spreads to choose from, it can be difficult to decide on the right one for you! You may even believe that if you don't have the proper spread, you won't be able to read the Tarot. This is not the case, as you will see in Chapter Four's demonstration of the one-card spread.

Tarot is about being creative and imaginative, and honing your intuition. When you design a spread, you engage in learning and construct your own path. After all, the Tarot is about The Fool developing his own identity and unique expression. You'll be doing the same thing. In other words, it will assist you in developing your own reading technique and forming a unique relationship with your deck.

The goal of creating a spread is to clear your mind, and to master asking the right questions to get good insights. A well-designed spread leads to a good reading. Tarot cards require context in order to convey a "narrative" through their visuals. Any insight provided will make sense.

Therefore, a spread is similar to a template in that it provides structure to insights. Moreover, it shapes the style of your readings by providing sequence or logic to intuitive insights. However, at first it may be helpful to follow a few established spreads to get a sense of how they work.

Steps for Creating a Tarot Spread:

If you search Pinterest for "Interview Tarot deck," you will find hundreds of spreads. However, the first thing you must do is determine the goal of the spread.

1. What is the goal of making a spread? (In the Interview Spread, our goal is to "meet" the new Tarot deck.)

2. Decide what you want to know. Write a brief paragraph and then divide it into a series of questions.

3. Keep your queries brief and to the point.

4. For each question, a card would be drawn. As a result, the number of questions may assist you in determining the number of cards in a spread.

5. Prepare your pen and Tarot journal to keep record of your discoveries.

THE INTERVIEW SPREAD

Purpose of interview: To find out if my Tarot card deck is a good match for me.

What I want to know: What is special about this particular deck, and what will I get out of it?

Recall a time when you had a job interview, or held one to recruit the right person for a position. The principle is the same. You are designing a spread around getting to know if a deck is a good match for you. You probably want to know what its features are, what its "specialty" is, what its "limitations" are, and whether you will "benefit by collaborating" with it. Eventually, what you really want to determine is whether it is a "good fit" for you and what you have in mind. Let's consider the keywords next:

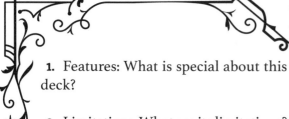

1. Features: What is special about this deck?

2. Limitations: What are its limitations?

3. Benefits: What I will learn by working with it?

4. Outcome: Are we a good fit?

Methodology

- Now that you know you have four questions, including the outcome, you know that your spread will require you to draw four cards.
- The next step is to try several methods of laying out four cards. Experiment with a layout that feels natural: left to right, for example, or in a row, or having the cards in a pile and drawing the first four. Alternatively, try the layout in figure 16 (page 105).
- Shuffle your cards to clear them (four to six times will do).
- Start shuffling the Major cards only (to begin with) until you are satisfied that they are clear.
- Shuffle the cards again, asking the first question in your mind: *"What is special about this deck?"* Then put the cards down.
- Either cut the deck once from left to right, which is the most popular way, placing the bottom half over the top one; or keep it simple by shuffling, repeating the question in your mind, and then randomly selecting the first card when you feel ready.
- Place the first card in position one, face down.
- Repeat the process for each question, placing each one face down to avoid influencing your expectation, then put down the remaining cards (you will notice that none of the cards are reversed. Since this is an initial spread, there is no need to do so).

Let's say you got the following cards:

House 1: Specialty = The Emperor

House 2: Limitations = Wheel of Fortune

House 3: Benefits = Justice

House 4: Outcome = The Lovers

Before you read the next section on interpreting the Interview Spread, stop and take time to interpret the cards you got, journaling your insights (or do a fresh Interview Spread reading using your own Tarot deck).

Interpretation of Interview Spread sample reading:

House 1: The specialty of this deck is The Emperor, which signifies structure, authority and stability (a grounded intuition) – a good indication that this deck has the authority to do what is required. It also indicates that it is probably used in a structure; for instance, the reading or spread needs to be structured, or it allows for complexity.

It seems that it can grow and develop with its user. Additionally, it indicates the need for the user to look after the well-being of their body and health, and maintain a harmonious home environment as represented by the number four.

House 2: The limitation of this deck is The Wheel of Fortune, which can indicate that it is quick to adapt, and can provide straightforward, direct answers as well as complex ones. It does not seem to be restricted by any limitation. So, it may be good to meditate on its cards, and use them as visual mantras as well.

House 3: The benefit of collaborating with this deck is the Justice card, signifying that results could be achieved swiftly and fairly. The benefit of working with it is learning the lesson offered by Justice, operating in a balanced manner, and delivering balanced and fair answers to the enquirer.

House 4: The outcome of working with this deck is signified by The Lovers, which is interesting! The Lovers represent a cooperative effort toward a harmonious result. This is a positive outcome card. The Lovers represents service to humanity, implying that this could be a harmonious relationship, that the user and the deck are a good match, and that the user may be able to help others reach their life goals using this deck. This implies that the deck can assist the user in their professional practice. However, like any other relationship, it has the potential to go either way! As a result, an additional card was naturally chosen to "follow" the outcome card and define the course of this partnership. The Fool is the fifth additional card to this spread.

First additional "follow-up" card: The Fool indicates that working with this deck will lead to an adventure. Despite the fact that the reader may not be familiar with the new deck, the extra "follow-up" card is encouraging the user to take a leap into the unknown, just like The Fool did! So, how will this "risk" pan out? The

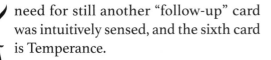

need for still another "follow-up" card was intuitively sensed, and the sixth card is Temperance.

Second additional "follow-up" card: Temperance implies a harmonic, balanced conclusion in improving the user's intuition, confirming that the user and the deck are a good match. Also, as the halo on the Temperance figure shows, the user is expected to use this deck in a balanced, responsible manner because the outcome is "illumination." Because water signifies the unconscious, feelings, and intuition, it is a fit for the reader's aim and can actually assist the reader in uncovering unconscious parts and bringing them to light.

This card resembles The Moon and The Star in that it features the water element, which is associated with unconscious qualities, such as dreams. This deck will aid the reader's self-development by balancing their unconscious side or psychic abilities with the logical structure provided by The Emperor, assuring that working with this deck will indeed be a great adventure!

Follow-up Cards

As you discovered in the Interview Spread above, the Tarot will sometimes give you an open-ended outcome card inviting you to investigate an issue further. The outcome could still go in either a positive or negative direction. This indicates that you do not yet have a final answer. A fluid outcome or result card depends on the nature of the card you draw, because certain Major (as well as Minor) cards have an open-ended interpretation, signifying a transition or the completion of a cycle and the beginning of a new one.

This is what makes the Tarot unique. It draws you in to investigate underlying currents and elements you are unaware of but should consider, particularly when a complex spread is used. The mystery deepens! Start practicing spreads and bring out the mystical sleuth within.

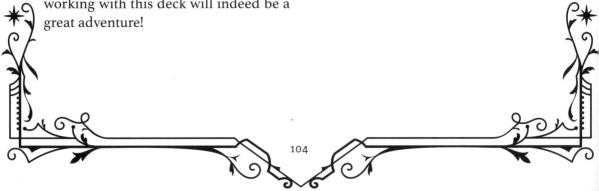

MY TAROT LEARNING JOURNAL

Date

Questions Asked

1. What am I going to learn about myself today?

2. What about ....
.... ?

3. What about ....
.... ?

Card Selected

1. The Tower ....

2. ....

3. ....

Layout

THE TOWER
NUMBER: 1   NUMBER   NUMBER

My Insights
(of card received,
or spread)

Perhaps I need to lose some assumptions that I am making. I can meditate some more on where sudden changes are likely to come and how to handle it when they do. ....
....
....
....
....
....
....
....
....
....
....
....
....
....
....
....
....
....

I ask for clear guidance from the source for my highest good. I am always protected.

Figure 16 Tarot journal entry.

	CARD	FOLLOW	INTERPRETING UPRIGHT OUTCOME CARD
0	THE FOOL	YES	YES: FOLLOW to check quality of the outcome.
1	THE MAGICIAN	–	YES.
2	THE HIGH PRIESTESS	YES	Not known yet; all info is not in place. FOLLOW.
3	THE EMPRESS	–	YES.
4	THE EMPEROR	–	YES: but requires a lot of effort.
5	THE HIEROPHANT	–	YES: destined for.
6	THE LOVERS	YES	Important decision. FOLLOW.
7	THE CHARIOT	–	YES: brilliant!
8	JUSTICE	YES	YES: FOLLOW to see the quality of the outcome.
9	THE HERMIT	YES	Not now. FOLLOW.
10	WHEEL OF FORTUNE	YES	Quick changes: FOLLOW.
11	STRENGTH	–	YES.
12	THE HANGED MAN	YES	Delays. Suspended.
13	DEATH	YES	Won't happen but FOLLOW.
14	TEMPERANCE	–	YES.
15	THE DEVIL	YES	NO: But FOLLOW to see why.
16	THE TOWER	YES	No answer—everything is changing. FOLLOW.
17	THE STAR	–	YES.
18	THE MOON	YES	You are in doubt at the time of the reading: FOLLOW.
19	THE SUN	–	YES.
21	JUDGMENT	YES	No decision is made at time of reading. Ask again another time. FOLLOW.
21	THE WORLD	–	YES. Expansion.

Figure 19 Table summarising follow-up of Major cards

	CARD	FOLLOW	INTERPRETING REVERSED OUTCOME CARD
0	THE FOOL	YES	NO: Bad risk. Serious mistake.
1	THE MAGICIAN	–	NO: Lack of information, communication, or inner abilities.
2	THE HIGH PRIESTESS	YES	NO.
3	THE EMPRESS	–	NO: Not really! Will not do well.
4	THE EMPEROR	–	NO: Too stressful.
5	THE HIEROPHANT	–	YES: Need unconventional approach.
6	THE LOVERS	YES	NO: Partnership will fail.
7	THE CHARIOT	–	NO: Don't force it. Let it go.
8	JUSTICE	YES	NO: Contract will be broken or will not happen.
9	THE HERMIT	YES	NO: Too confused.
10	WHEEL OF FORTUNE	YES	No decision yet.
11	STRENGTH	–	NO: No initiative, inner resources, or good will.
12	THE HANGED MAN	YES	Delays: Follow.
13	DEATH	YES	NO: Final, you can't avoid it.
14	TEMPERANCE	–	NO: Matters are out of balance.
15	THE DEVIL	YES	NO: But follow.
16	THE TOWER	YES	NO. FOLLOW.
17	THE STAR	–	Will happen, but may be delayed.
18	THE MOON	YES	You are not getting what you want: Follow.
19	THE SUN	–	YES: But can be a compromise. Follow.
21	JUDGMENT	YES	NO: Judgment is against you.
21	THE WORLD	–	NO

CHAPTER FOUR

TAROT SPREADS

READING METHODOLOGY

The spread you use is determined by what you're seeking advice abut. Start your session with a brief invocation, a prayer, or just stating your goal to set the tone and create a connection with the cards.

Spend some time thinking about your questions. Writing down what you wish to inquire about is a fantastic way to get your concerns out of your head (see the section on The Interview Spread). Next, determine which spread you will use; is your question about a short- or long-term prospect.

- Separate the two arcana and shuffle your Major cards in a single direction to clear their energy. Keep shuffling while focusing on your question.
- The first time you shuffle, you want to clear the deck. As you shuffle, you might want to repeat the phrase "clear... clear." Then shuffle again, this time focusing on your question.
- As you shuffle, keep the question in mind and reverse a total of two cards from the Major Arcana any time you feel like it. The purpose of reversing cards is to expose important concerns that require your attention. Your subconscious mind will guide you in drawing the cards. If you see any reversed cards in a spread, it indicates a part of your development that needs your focus. They will frequently indicate "the way out" of an unfavorable situation (refer to the table on reversed card meanings in Chapter One).

- Start combining Major and Minor cards in the spread of your choice. Typically, you would begin by arranging the main cards first, then repeat the process to select the Minor cards. The Minor cards are placed in the same order as the Major cards, according to the spread's sequence. This is known as "covering" the Major card since each Minor card covers, or complements, the meaning of the Major card it is associated with in that position.
- Draw the cards with your non-dominant hand, to stay connected to your intuition.
- Focus on the Major cards first, which represent major events and cycles of transformation. Track the story that the Major cards are presenting. Consider reinterpreting that story by including the interpretation and significance of the Minor cards in their respective order. What additional insights do they inspire, and how are their meanings associated with each other?
- This helps you structure your reading by

considering the big picture, or general outlook, first, before you move into details. Additionally, it may offer a more accurate reading in the context of the spread. Place the deck face down in front of you whenever you are ready. With your dominant hand, fan the cards out in a line, and take a moment to release any attachments to an expected outcome. This will help you receive unbiased wisdom from your cards. Keep breathing calmly and stay grounded and open to receiving the cards' counsel.

When you get used to shuffling, you might find that you do not need to fan the cards out by laying them down. You can randomly draw the required cards as you hold them in your hand, and place each in its respective order before you draw the next one.

The steps to undertake when starting a reading session are outlined below:
- Determine what you need help with.
- Figure out whether it is a short- or long-term issue.
- Phrase your questions mindfully.
- Choose a spread.
- Separate Major cards from Minor cards.
- Shuffle the cards in one direction to clear them.

- Concentrate on a single question.
- Reverse two Major cards only.
- Put the deck down.
- Select cards at random (don't overthink it!).
- Place the selected cards according to your chosen spread, one card at a time.
- Repeat, using the procedure above if you intend to use the Minor cards in the same spread.

PHRASING YOUR QUESTION

People frequently seek spiritual advice while they are struggling in their prosaic, earthly lives. So when reading for others, don't underestimate your inquiry or the seeker's question. Any seemingly insignificant question could open a door to further "enlightenment" or self-awareness. This is why taking time to clarify the question is important. Use simple and succinct sentences.

Interpreting Tarot Spreads

No matter which spread you choose, the end card, also known as the result or outcome card, occasionally requires an additional card to follow it. The follow-up card clarifies the outcome of the spread. For example, if your result card is The Fool, it indicates that you are about to start in a new direction or take an unknown risk. You have no idea how it will pan out. In such a case, you would draw an additional card to evaluate whether you received a decisive answer. Another example of an open-ended outcome card is the Wheel of Fortune. It symbolizes speedy and unforeseen changes in your situation. Therefore, you follow it with an additional card (after you shuffle again) to determine the nature of the changes to come.

Moreover, when a Tarot card appears reversed in a reading, it has a somewhat different meaning than the upright one. In general, if you focus on the card's imagery, or use the "walk into the picture" technique described earlier, you will be able to deduce its inverted meaning (and of course you have the table summarizing those meanings). A reversed card emerges in a spread to draw your attention to underlying currents or elements which you are not aware of at the time of the reading. Even though the follow-up can be used with any Tarot spread, drawing four or more cards will confuse the outcome! Stop, and return to asking about that issue later.

What is also interesting is that the seeker's desire for a specific outcome can occasionally be so intense that it influences the cards they draw. In that instance, take the cards into your hands, shuffle them to clear them, and then draw the appropriate number of cards on the seeker's behalf. If you work online, you are probably already doing this. It makes no difference to the reading as long as you (as the reader) are centered and maintain your connection to the "highest source" of guidance.

This strategy provides structure to the reading while also facilitating the interpretation of more complex spreads and developing your intuition. Insights without context are like a boat with no rudder or oars—not very helpful! Moreover, the purpose of a Tarot reading is to provide insights as well as enhance your understanding. So you need to capture the essence of the Tarot cards' advice, whether for yourself or someone else. In other words, you need to be able to integrate all the information by starting with the details and gradually weaving a "Tarot tapestry" stitch by stitch. Let's do that next.

Keep in mind that when Minor cards are used to supplement Major cards in the same spread, it is recommended that you reverse two Major cards and five

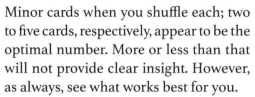

Minor cards when you shuffle each; two to five cards, respectively, appear to be the optimal number. More or less than that will not provide clear insight. However, as always, see what works best for you.

Additionally, you can select all the cards of the spread and place them according to the spread's template, either all at once or by shuffling again before choosing the next. It doesn't make a difference. If you are a beginner, however, shuffling and repeating each question in your head before you select the card for the next position may help focus your mind and memorize what the card positions, or houses, stand for.

THE ONE-CARD SPREAD

When you're unsure how to formulate a question, imagine or pretend that your deck is chatting with you, asking, "What is 'your story' leading to your query?" For example, you may write, *"This is a big day for me because ... and I'd like to know how it will turn out. Is it as important as I believe it is, or a passing opportunity that I should miss?"* Or if you are starting a new project or business, *"This is the official start of my new business, and I'm curious about how the first three years will pan out."*

To get your mind unstuck, you can just shuffle your cards, asking, *"What about the issue I have in mind?"* before selecting one card to get your thoughts unstuck. The first card you draw will set the ball rolling. Your mind will prompt you to ask further questions as you consider its meaning. This one-card method will assist you in phrasing any subsequent queries and determining the best spread to use. Let's try it using Major cards only; shuffle and reverse two cards.

Examples of how to phrase questions for a one-card spread:

- What do I need to know about the issue I have in mind? (meeting, project, job offer, property, person)
- What does my heart tell me about ...?
- What is holding me back from ...?
- Why am I experiencing this obstacle now?
- What will help me overcome this situation?
- What is my relationship with ... about?
- How will ... develop?

Sample reading 1: *Dan is in his mid-sixties, lost his beloved wife about five years ago, and is wondering if he will meet someone.*

Question: *"What about Dan having a meaningful, fulfilling relationship with the right partner?"*

Card: Temperance

Interpretation: Temperance represents emotional healing, symbolized by the angel figure pouring the water between two cups. It relates to healing Dan's grief, and indicates that he will experience a nurturing, stable, and harmonious relationship again. He delighted with the outcome of his reading!

Sample Reading 2: Susan, who is a therapist, became acquainted with a healer whom she worked with from time to time. He proposed that they work together; however, she was confused at this sudden opportunity and wondered what it was about. She had many questions in mind, so we decided to ask:

Question: *"What about the issue I have in mind?"*

Card: The Hierophant

Interpretation: This card represents spiritual matters, as well as someone who speaks their truth and is spiritually aware. It denotes someone who wants to serve others and most likely operates ethically, as The Hierophant represents accessible greater wisdom. It might be describing

Susan or the healer, but it is a positive omen in any scenario. Susan, on the other hand, wanted to delve more into the guidance provided by this card. She decided to shuffle and draw another card.

Second question: *"Why is this healer interested in collaborating? What are his intentions?"*

Card: The Hermit

Interpretation: The Hermit denotes more study, more knowledge, and a selfless individual who "lights" the way for others. The Hermit can also signify a recluse, someone who works alone, withdraws into his own spiritual world, and presumably avoids the trappings of materialism. It refers to the male healer who wanted to collaborate with Susan. It also provided an answer to her inquiry and symbolized the healer's motivation. He wants to teach Susan, or share healing information with her; as The Hermit, he has no ulterior motive other than to serve people. Despite being happy with this answer, she wanted to dig more, and drew another card.

Third Question: *"How will this collaboration develop?"*

Card: Justice

Interpretation: Justice denotes formal legalization of the collaboration. They might both sign an agreement, showing that this collaboration will be a fair and just one. Susan was delighted at this prospect and became eager to know more. She asked to draw another card.

Fourth Question: *"What type of formal collaboration will this be?"*

Card: The Magician

Interpretation: The Magician represents the possibility of starting a project or partnership. It also implies that information will be transferred, as shown by the white "communication" rod The Magician is holding toward Spirit, and the finger of his other hand pointing downwards, bringing the information down. It also reflects Susan's inner abilities and potential as a person who has everything she needs within her; this is symbolized by the "four elements" objects on the table in front of The Magician. The exchange of knowledge might be progressive, as symbolized by the infinity symbol over The Magician's head and the Snake biting its tail around

his waist. While meditating on the "belt," an image of a snake shedding its skin flashed clairvoyantly.

Perhaps the collaboration will take place in stages. It demonstrates the growing nature of the collaboration. In any event, because The Magician also represents two-way communication, Susan and the healer may soon communicate, most likely via text or email (information travels quickly between the hands of The Magician). The outcome of the spread is that a collaboration will be beneficial, and that Susan is capable of assessing her situation as it unfolds. She can take this collaboration as far as she sees fit if it continues to suit her goals. In any case, she has everything to gain by working with this healer.

Reading Summary: Several queries were spontaneously prompted. A four-card spread proved to be the most effective reading strategy. It is an example of how to clarify an issue as well as how to construct a spread. Furthermore, it demonstrates how Major cards on their own can provide straight and unambiguous counsel. You can modify and apply the one-card strategy to create subsequent spreads (refer to the Interview Spread in the preceding chapter).

Sample Reading 3: In this sample reading, we will begin with the Major cards in the spread and progress to the Minor cards. It will give you an idea of how they can provide more information, adding details to a reading. Consider separating the Major and Minor cards. Shuffle the Major cards first, reversing just two cards, and then draw a card. Repeat the procedure with the Minor card, reverse five cards while shuffling, and "cover" the Major card with the Minor card.

John's 60th birthday is approaching. This is a big milestone. He was reflecting on his life and wanted some insights on what is coming up. What does he have to look forward to, and what would be the main focus?

Question: *"What is the significance of John's 60th birthday?"*

Card 1: The Sun

Interpretation: Woo-hoo! This is one of the best Tarot cards to receive for such a question. The Sun denotes a new cycle of renewal and growth. The Sun is card number 19, nearing the end of The Fool's journey, signifying that he has undergone a cycle of transformation and perhaps some rough times. However, The Sun now heralds a joyous life. Whatever he has been struggling with is nearing its conclusion. On a personal level, he is beginning to feel more comfortable in his skin. He is not holding back, as he may have been in the past; he is looking forward to this new cycle.

This is symbolized by the naked child riding the gray horse of spiritual transformation. Moreover, the orange banner waved by the Sun child denotes renewed vigor; John could very well meet someone or travel abroad. The difficult emotional period he may have gone through (indicated by the preceding card to The Sun, The Moon) helped him clear all the cobwebs and face unconscious fears. He is now heading toward The Sun, and as ready as a transformed Fool can be for a new adventure, symbolized by the red feather on his head—which the Fool was wearing at the beginning of the journey. John will not be retiring from life. There's a wonderful adventure waiting for him.

To demonstrate how the Minor cards can support the Major reading, we are going to assume that John wanted to know the main character or theme of this new cycle. If you were conducting this reading, you would shuffle the Minor cards, (reversing five cards to add complexity and more information). Then you would select one card.

Minor Card: Queen of Cups

Interpretation: The Minor card John selected was a water element, the Queen of Cups. This adds more information, enforcing that his "bad cycle" was about healing his unconscious feelings. Perhaps he suffered a loss or the end of a relationship, or he had fears about entering a new relationship. In any case, this card symbolizes that he has overcome challenges. As a man receiving this card, it denotes that his duality is well balanced and that he is in touch with his feminine side and his intuition. It is a calm image of authority.

The cup that the Queen of Cups is offering John is a large one, denoting happiness, joy, and harmony in the next cycle. It could be describing a romantic partner; in this case, she would be nurturing and supportive. The relationship would be a harmonious and well-balanced one. The Queen is sitting on a throne away from the shore, suggesting that he might meet this woman abroad, or that they might move abroad.

THE THREE-CARD SPREAD

The three-card spread is quite versatile and can be adapted to any level of inquiry, from the mundane to the profound. It is also ideal to obtain quick answers to long-term issues such as, "How will my marriage turn out?"

Moreover, you can create your own three-card spreads that correspond to what you wish to know. See the previous example of creating the Interview Spread.

Figure 19 shows some variations of the three-card spread, which you can adapt to suit your goal. For example, you can create a three-card template for personal growth, career growth, a fulfilling relationship, or interpreting your dreams.

Additionally, you can combine the Minor cards with this spread for additional information, as in the sample reading below. What you need to decide first is what each of the three "houses" or positions stands for. Figure 19 is a template you can vary to create your own three-card spread:

Sample Reading 1: Lee is a young man who has recently graduated from university. But his excitement about starting his career and independence was short-lived. The start of the Covid-19 pandemic and lockdown made it difficult for him to find work or launch his career in the field of film production. Currently, he has an OK job that he found after lockdown restrictions were lifted. However, he's concerned about what will happen to the career he is passionate about.

Question: *"What about Lee's career in film production?"*

Card 1: Underlying issue—The Devil

The Devil is about becoming enslaved to attitudes or habits that are no longer benefiting us. Their sole purpose is to divert our attention from our goals and from expressing our potential. This card represents Lee's unconscious pessimistic attitude, which was most likely impacted by lockdown. Perhaps he still feels imprisoned by the "underworld" and the confining negativity and despair. His mental state has not changed, despite the fact that his life has returned to "normal" in recent months. The following card hints at how Lee can ease his way forward.

Card 2: Factors to be considered—Strength

Fortitude and perseverance are the qualities of Strength. It suggests that Lee has what it takes to overcome "beastly," stifling conditions, no matter how daunting they appear. He has a tremendous reservoir of strength, charisma, and skill inside him to conquer his issue and achieve his goal. All he has to do to activate this inner strength is perceive himself as an adult with the right to pursue the future he desires. Furthermore, he appears to have innate creative potential, as shown by the infinity symbol above Strength. Lee may lack experience, but he has what it takes to succeed in a field that he is passionate about. He'll never run out of creative ideas! This intrinsic ability, however, signifies confidence, which he must allow himself to reveal and express, especially when meeting potential employers, as the following card suggests.

Card 3: Outcome—The Lovers

The Lovers is about collaboration and relationships, and it portends an upcoming interview, which could be the opportunity Lee seeks. It appears that he will find the ideal employer, with whom he will get along and enjoy a pleasant work atmosphere in which he will be nurtured and supported. The Lovers signify a choice between two options. Should he take this new opportunity when it arises, or stay in his current position? A follow-up is required.

Follow-up Card 1: Justice

This card represents a legal agreement. The future is looking brighter for Lee! The interview indicated by The Lovers card may result in an agreement and an employment contract. Is this contract a sensible and positive one? To determine the outcome, an additional follow-up card is required.

Follow-up Card 2: The Sun

The Sun affirms Lee's success and happiness as a result of signing a contract. The sunflowers imply that this could happen before the conclusion of the current summer. As the flag the "Sun child" is flying symbolizes, Lee is reminded to exhibit his passion and fervor in his job. The next job will help Lee forge his career and reputation in the field, as The Sun signifies. Moreover, The Sun also indicates the conclusion of a transformative cycle (giving up a negative mindset) and preparation for the next one, in which Lee will be totally fulfilled!

Reading Summary: Looking at all the cards together, it appears Lee is undergoing a transformation; he must believe in himself and abandon the cautious, pessimistic attitude he may unconsciously assume to be realistic. He must allow his creative spirit to shine through, and freely express his confidence and passion. He must persevere in his search for the right job, because an opportunity is on its way. A

contract will be signed, and Lee will enjoy working in that environment. Success is guaranteed.

Sample Reading 2: In the following reading, Major and Minor cards were used. Andrea had a crush on Thomas, who had been sending her confusing signals for approximately two years. For a few months, neither of them defined or acknowledged their relationship. When she confronted Thomas, he went berserk. She felt exhausted and preoccupied by this so-called romance, and she could not figure it out. What was the purpose of it?

Card 1: The nature of the issue— Death

Death inspires a variety of interpretations on a number of levels when it comes to the question of relationships. It depicts the point of no return, the end of the old and the beginning of the new. It might apply to both Andrea and her friend. However, since she is the one inquiring, let's start with her. Death suggests that her life is undergoing a metamorphosis that could not have been avoided. The fact that the card is upright indicates that she did not resist this tough adjustment (the reader did not ask for more details). Death suggests that there was a sacrifice, that the previous "king" was crushed by Death's horse. As a result, this relationship is unlike any she has had before—she is in uncharted waters. Was the relationship "dead" and over before it even started?

Card 2: The benefit of the relationship—The Hermit

The Hermit represents solitude. Perhaps it is inviting Andrea to withdraw and reflect on what she is going through, or implying that she needs to be alone to reflect. It also implies that more information will be revealed. Perhaps her aloneness gave this issue more significance; nonetheless, she wanted to find out more. The connection with Thomas also initiated a spiritual lesson, or learning phase, according to The Hermit. The Hermit is card number nine, denoting the end or completion of a process (of adjustment), right before starting a new one on a higher level (nine moves into ten, which represents fulfillment). On another level, while being in a relationship, she feels alone, as The Hermit suggests. She may be unknowingly retreating from life (because of whatever circumstance Death brought about). She is advised to investigate whether she was unconsciously avoiding romance by distracting herself with one that does not appear to be promising (no "love" cards appeared so far).

Card Three: The Outcome – The Hanged Man

This card denotes another type of transition or change; Andrea needs to see the matter from an entirely different perspective. The progression of the three cards indicates that this crush instigated the completion of a personal development she was undergoing prior to meeting him. The final step in this cycle is to step back and see things differently. The issue does not seem to be about their relationship, but about her finding out what kind of relationship she was after.

Was she after a fulfilling one? Or was any relationship better than no relationship? Considering the three cards together, perhaps it was The Hermit who did not wish to come out of his solitude either. In any case, as she "hangs upside down" like The Hanged Man, she will see the light and change her perspective, as the halo around The Hanged Man indicates. To see how her transformation will unfold, two additional follow-up cards were required.

First Additional Follow-up Card— The Lovers

Andrea's life appears to be building up to a decision, possibly between two people. What she seeks is a balanced, supportive

1.   2.   3.

Figure 20 The 3-Card Spread layout

relationship that will help her achieve her goals (represented by the mountain in the distance, behind the couple). Her relationship with Thomas lacks the emotional security that comes from being with the correct person in a balanced relationship. A further follow-up card is necessary to find out what the decision is.

Second Additional Follow-up Card— Strength

Strength is about training primal instincts to evolve to a higher level of awareness, one where Andrea will be connected with herself and her true feelings. She will be able to appreciate her own charm, beauty, and strength. Her newfound self-worth will end this state of confusion and distraction over a non-working relationship that distracted her for too long. The new level of mastery she will attain will bring about self-healing and regeneration (since efforts are ill-spent nurturing the wrong relationship). She will have the fortitude to overcome the situation until she meets her equal.

If, on the other hand, The Hermit represents Thomas, he may be going through a period of self-growth in which he chooses not to be with anyone. The pressure of having to decide may be what freaked him out. He wasn't ready to leave his seclusion. Intuitively, he appears to want to travel light, like a hermit, at this moment, rather than share life's journey with a companion.

To add an additional layer of information, the cards were shuffled and three Minor Arcana cards were chosen, one for each of the first three cards, in respective order one to three.

3-CARD SPREAD TEMPLATE

CARD 1	CARD 2	CARD 3
Past	Present	Future
Body	Mind	Spirit
Subconscious	Conscious	Higher wisdom
Underlying issue	Factors to be considered	Outcome
Issue	What is blocking me?	Outcome
Strengths	Weaknesses	Outcome
Nature of issue	Benefit	Outcome
Nature of issue	Risks involved	Outcome
Where I am	Where I need to be	Outcome (best version)

Figure 21 The 3-Card Spread, sample reading 1

Minor Card 1: The nature of the issue—King of Pentacles

The King of Pentacles represents a kind and loving person who is well balanced and stable, and understands the spiritual wisdom behind creating an abundant material life without any attachments or hang-ups. He is a man who is comfortable and knows where he belongs. He is also at the end of his growth cycle (pentacles); in other words, he is accomplished. This does not seem to correspond to Thomas, the person Andrea is crushing over. Since the Minor card falls underneath the Death card, it relates to the previous man Andrea was in relationship with, which ended.

Minor Card 2: The Benefit – Nine of Pentacles

Andrea is represented by the figure of the Nine of Pentacles enjoying her bountiful surroundings. Because it falls under The Hermit card, it explains why Andrea is advised to "withdraw" from this relationship. Her career ambitions and aspirations are about to be realized (number 9), and she has to focus on her career. This is a positive card that also represents why the relationship was not meant to work. Andrea was most likely disregarding herself, her profession, and other joyful

1	2	3	Follow-up card 1	Follow-up card 2
Underlying Issue	Factors to be considered	The outcome		

Figure 22 Lee's reading

areas of her life. She has clearly achieved something substantial, as evidenced by the accomplished woman represented in the Nine of Pentacles. Her interest in Thomas pushed her out of her loneliness and made her focus on herself, her appearance (a well-dressed figure in exquisite clothes), and her career.

Minor Card 3: The Outcome – Four of Pentacles

The Four of Pentacles, the outcome card, is about creating financial stability. It is advising Andrea that what she needs to view differently today is that her priority is her business, which should be developed now. Furthermore, in response to her query about relationships (consider the cards before and after this one), the ideal partner would be one who supports and encourages Andrea to pursue her career goals (The Lovers). Her emotional stability will aid in the establishment of her financial security. She is also advised to organize her finances (number 4) in order to achieve financial security by reinvesting some of her profits back into her business and saving for the future (notice how the figure in the Four of Pentacles is holding the pentacle like the wheel of fortune; money needs to circulate or keep flowing). The financial wheel will keep turning if you save and reinvest.

Minor Follow-Up Card 1: Eight of Pentacles

This card shows that Andrea possesses (or has the potential to acquire) abilities that can strengthen and improve her income. When these two cards are read in sequence, they signal that she can attain financial success and expand her business by mastering a skill directly related to it. Six Pentacles are displayed on the wooden beam in front of her, indicating that she possesses the right skills, which she can expand on. All she has to do is keep applying those skills (the cards are indicating how her business can grow). The second Minor card implies that she manages her own business, rather than being employed. This is depicted by the figure of the woman who has achieved a certain level of success in the Nine of Pentacles.

Because the first Minor follow-up card is below The Lovers card, the partner she meets may be prepared to support her in improving her business and directing her skills. The four Pentacle cards form the spread so far, and "cover" the Major cards; this indicates that Andrea's attention should be on her finances, rather than her love life. That was something she wasn't aware of. The developmental cycle, if you will, is about finance and money, which Andrea should think about before entering into a romantic relationship. This is what the Hanged Man card is alluding to. If you like, this is the "season" for growing finances (before love).

Minor Follow-up Card 2: Nine of Wands

The message of the Nine of Wands is fortitude and perseverance. Drawing this card is fortunate, because it covers the Strength card in the spread, and thus reinforces it. The card is showing Andrea that she has the fortitude to go through the current phase, and that if she sticks with her business and steadily grows it, she will be able to overcome any difficulties that appear insurmountable. The eight wands behind the figure represent Andrea's struggles.

The figure holding one wand only denotes that Andrea feels ill-equipped to meet those challenges. Moreover, the facial expression on the figure enforces how worried she must feel. The eight wands behind the figure in the card also indicate that she has been through a lot, which gave her the experience she needed to deal with struggles. However, the worst is over since the eight wands are already behind the figure, not facing him. Andrea is at a good point in her life. She has the experience, strength, and skills needed to continue her journey.

Reading Summary: Andrea had a difficult time in both her business and her love life. There is a sense that she is beginning a new life, and at a definite cut-off with her previous life. She wants to know why she has such strong feelings for Thomas, despite the fact that their relationship hasn't truly grown over the last two years. What is the point of this experience? Her cards indicated that in order to understand what she is going through, she needed to change her perspective and recognize what she was unaware of. Her romantic interest in Thomas assisted her in refocusing on herself, coming out of her withdrawal after suffering a loss and recognizing that she was not feeling fulfilled.

What she was looking for was emotional stability to propel her development, which she was not receiving from Thomas. Thomas could be going through something similar, and the way he is coping is by refusing to engage in relationships. He may be alleviating his load by not taking on the responsibility of supporting anyone else. Instead, the cards encouraged her to concentrate on growing her business, which is what will bring her fulfillment right now. She has invested in and accomplished a lot with it.

Despite her prior difficulties, she is now well-equipped to thrive. Her efforts must be focused on honing her talents in order to expand her business. Fulfilling

1	2	3	Follow-up card **1**	Follow-up card **2**
Underlying Issue	Factors to be considered	The outcome		

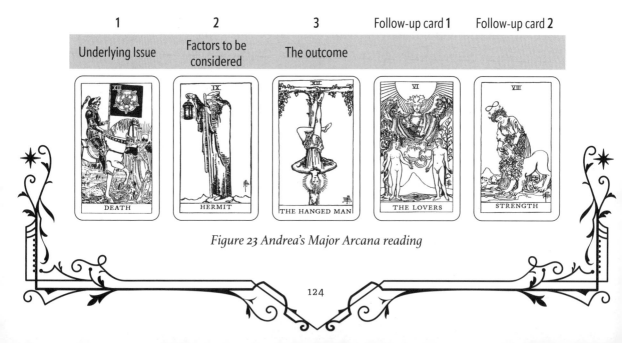

Figure 23 Andrea's Major Arcana reading

her ambitions is what will bring her out of her isolation. She will then be prepared to share and enjoy a fulfilling, caring relationship with a supportive and loving partner.

YES-OR-NO SPREAD

When to use this spread: When you need a simple yes or no answer, use this spread. Because the answer truly hangs in the balance, the Justice card is placed in the background as a reminder that the outcome is critical, a just and fair one that will have consequences. When the outcome card is inconclusive, draw a follow-up card as explained earlier in Chapter Three under *What a Tarot Reading Is* (page 98).

When your inquiry is about legal matters, however, you can use the Judgment card as a background instead of the Justice card.

In this spread, you can use only the Major cards. There's no need to cover with Minor cards, as the former will provide decisive answers. As discussed earlier, questions need to be clear, so double-barreled questions will give a confused reading. Instead, just ask *"What about this issue?"* or *"Will I succeed in …?"* and not *"Will I buy this house or not?"*

Sample Reading 1: *"What about John's physical health after surgery?"*

Cards 1: Background—The Tower

Card 2: Turning Point—The World

Card 3: Outcome—The Moon

Follow-up card: Strength

Interpretation: The Tower shows that John's illness abruptly changed for the worse. The World card, on the other hand, suggests that he will have a positive turnaround. Finally, Strength denotes recovery and the body rallying. The spread indicates that John will regain his health.

Sample Reading 2: *"What about Charlotte's relationship with Mark?"*

Card 1: Background—The Star

Card 2: Turning Point—Death

Card 3: Outcome—The Lovers

Follow-up card 1: Judgment

Follow-up card 2: The Magician

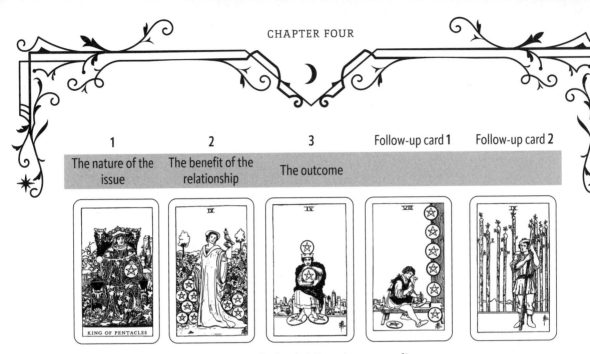

1	2	3	Follow-up card 1	Follow-up card 2
The nature of the issue	The benefit of the relationship	The outcome		

Figure 24 Andrea's Minor Arcana reading

Interpretation: The relationship's background is The Star, which indicates that this relationship will provide healing and emotional balance to both lovers. Death and Judgment, on the other hand, are significant transformation cards. They indicate that both parties will go through major transformations because of this partnership, which is not to imply that this relationship is undesirable because the cards are stacked against it. In fact, the opposite is true: In order for this relationship to work, both Charlotte and Mark will have to confront the issues they did not address individually in the past. If you will, the relationship serves as a vital catalyst propelling further personal development. It urges them to confront and resolve their own issues.

The Lovers card implies that this connection will allow both of them achieve balance and harmony as a result of realizing that neither of them can continue in any relationship unless they endure the "Death" of previous attitudes or preconceptions about what a partnership is. The follow-up Judgment card represents more transformation, or purification. Both will go through this process in order to remove any hurdles preventing them from having a healthy, positive relationship.

Finally, The Magician verifies that this relationship will be successful if both parties communicate openly and honestly. Being clear about their needs and working through their individual issues will reap dividends. It will be a rewarding, balanced, and supportive, as well as stimulating, partnership.

Sample Reading 3: Tamara and Neil are in their mid-thirties. They live in a small apartment in New York with their son, who is four. Both would like to have another child, which would require moving to a larger home. They put their apartment on the market, and want to know when the move will be possible.

Question: *"What about Tamara and Neil moving to a larger home within the next three months?" or "What about the sale of Tamara and Neil's apartment within three months?"*

Card 1: Background—Temperance

Card 2: Turning Point—The Lovers

Card 3: Outcome—The Hierophant

Interpretation: Temperance indicates that the timing is favorable for this decision to happen. There will be an agreement or understanding that Tamara and Neil have made the correct decision to sell and relocate. The Lovers represent a choice between two options. This can refer to a decision between two buyers for their current home, or a choice between two homes for them to purchase. It is a beneficial card, because it signals that a sale will take place and that alternatives are open. The Hierophant, the outcome card, is a resounding yes! So it appears that a move is feasible within the next three months.

We hope that *The Book of Tarot* has inspired you to begin your Tarot adventure as courageously as The Fool did, to go through life seeking wisdom as boldly as he did, and that your readings will restore seekers' self-will and inspire them to take a leap into the unknown—where fulfillment lies.

The End

Further reading

Other books of by Sahar Huneidi-Palmer

Create Your Own Flower Tarot

Tarot for Self-Transformation

Author recommendations

Tarot—Alice Ekrek

Intuitive Tarot—Brigit Esselmont

The Ultimate Guide to the Tarot—Johannes Fiebig

Tarot for Yourself—Mary K Greer

Tarot Plain and Simple—Anthony Louis

Seventy-eight Degrees of Wisdom—Rachel Pollack

The Pictorial Key to the Tarot—A.E. Waite

Author online

Website: saharhuneidi.com

Twitter: @saharhuneidi

Podcast: Unbox The Podcast: Live Your Best Life with Sahar